GUNS
of the
OLD WEST

Above: *Colt Single Action Army revolver,*
.45in caliber, and shoulder holster, both 1890s.

GUNS *of the* OLD WEST

AN ILLUSTRATED HISTORY

DEAN K. BOORMAN

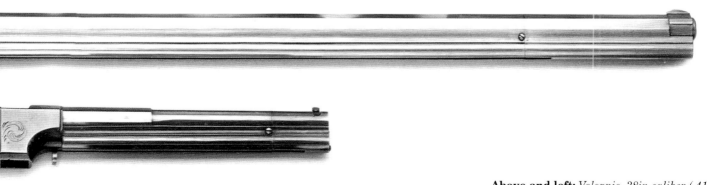

Above and left: *Volcanic .38in caliber (.41 cartridge) 25-shot carbine and, below it, Smith & Wesson .38in caliber (.41 cartridge) 10-shot pistol.*

THE LYONS PRESS

A SALAMANDER BOOK

Published in the United States by The Lyons Press
Guilford, CT 06437
www.lyonspress.com
An imprint of The Globe Pequot Press

© Salamander Books Ltd. 2002

A member of **Chrysalis** Books plc

ISBN 1-58574-702-5

1 2 3 4 5 6 7 8 9 10

THE AUTHOR

Dean K. Boorman is president of the prestigious Armor and Arms Club of New York, formed in 1921, believed to be the "oldest club of collectors in the Western hemisphere," and affiliated to the New York Metropolitan Museum of Art. He is also a member of the prestigious American Society of Arms Collectors, and has written for both the American Society and the Armor and Arms Club. He is also author of two successful Salamander books, *The History of Colt Firearms*, and *The History of Winchester Firearms*.

CREDITS

Project Manager: Ray Bonds
Designer: Heather Moore, Mitchell Print and Publishing Solutions
Colour reproduction: Anorax Imaging Ltd
Printed and bound in Taiwan

ACKNOWLEDGMENTS

The publishers thank all the museums and private collectors for so graciously providing firearms and other artifacts for photography, in particular the Buffalo Bill Historical Center, Cody, Wyoming, and the Gene Autry Western Heritage Museum; and also G. Allan Brown for permission to reproduce photographs from R. L. Wilson's fine book *Winchester: An American Legend*.

Above: *Famed Colt Peacemaker/Frontier with double-loop holster and belt.*

CONTENTS

PREFACE

Iam pleased to introduce Dean Boorman's handsome and informative new book on Western firearms. This follows up on his previous two books, The History of Colt Firearms and of Winchester to provide an overall picture of the vital part played by firearms in this glamorous and pivotal period of American history. In addition to Dean Boorman's text, which emphasizes how the guns were developed and used, the book is distinguished by its extensive color photos. I am

impressed by how these can bring the guns to life on the book's pages.

I constantly emphasize the relation between firearms development and Western expansion. A direct correlation between the explosion in firearms manufacturing and technology and the westward expansion of the United States is very evident. As gun designs became better and more practical, the "taming of the West" became a task that was accomplished with grit, determination, and a reliable firearm.

We all admire the handsome design and technological ingenuity of arms like Colts and Winchesters. This book puts these in the perspective of the turbulent times in which these firearms and those of other makers were developed and used. While there is a great deal of mythology in the common perception of these times, debunked in the book, the reality is sufficiently romantic to satisfy the most avid fans of Western movies!

I hope the readers of this book will

Below: *Factory engraved and pearl-inlaid Winchester Model 1873 once owned by trail-blazing entrepreneur Charles Goodnight, together with a cowboy's rawhide hand-braided riata from the late 1800s.*

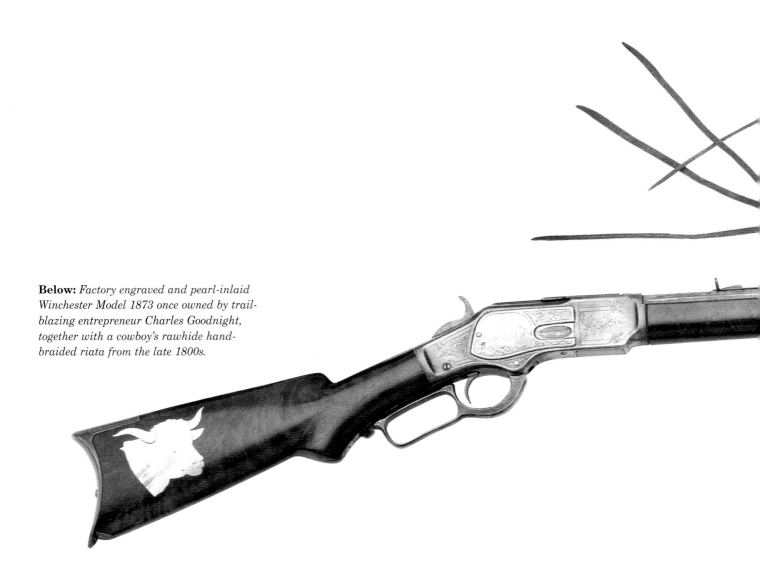

be inspired to come to see the guns themselves at museums like mine or at gun shows and similar venues, but in any event, that their understanding will be stimulated of this essential part of our common past.

Philip Schreier,
Curator of Educational Programs
of the National Firearms Museum,
National Rifle Association

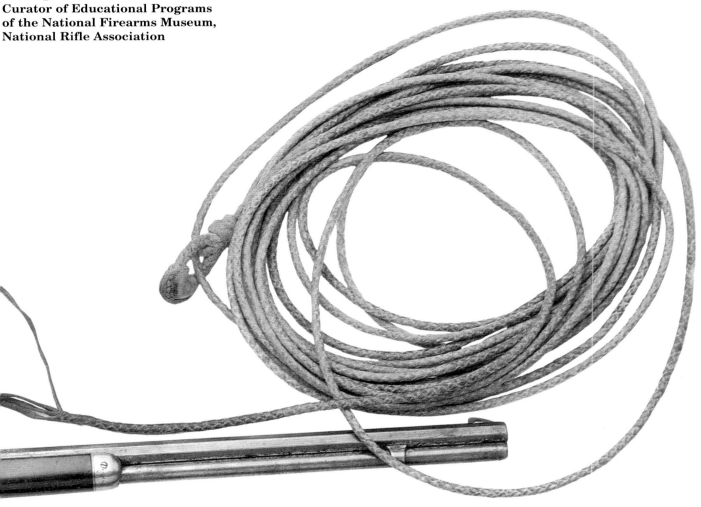

INTRODUCTION

Firearms are associated with the Old West more than any other era of American history. This may be attributed to competing claims by Colt and Winchester as "The Guns That Won The West," and to the tradition, now somewhat dimmed, of Western movies. Today, a number of firearms enthusiasts have even created the sport of "Cowboy Action Shooting," where the participants use original or replica Western rifles and pistols in make-believe settings, while they adopt Western nicknames and clothing.

However, the interest and significance of the firearms used on the Western frontier go beyond romantic stereotypes. Firearms were primarily tools used for hunting for food and for defense against hostile Indians and lawless elements. Gunfights were the exception rather than the rule, but drew attention in tabloids and dime novels just as crime stories do in today's news.

The firearms themselves were part of a technological revolution which transformed the United States from a small group of former colonies to the world's major industrial and military power. These arms, coming from a partnership of Yankee know-how in the industrial Northeast and the pioneering ideal which led to the settlement of the West, are true expressions of the American spirit.

The intention in this book is to provide an overview of all the significant types of firearms that were used on the Western frontier. In doing this, the emphasis is on letting these handsome artifacts speak for themselves through pictures, which traditionally are worth more than many words! At the same time, an effort is made to place the guns in the context of the time in which they were used. This was a most significant period for the United States, and the tradition of an open, pioneering society also advancing technologically is still a model for us today.

The "Old West" is considered here to have begun with the Louisiana Purchase in 1803 together with the Lewis and Clark expedition in 1804 to 1806, and to end in 1890 with the Battle of Wounded Knee and the Government's declaration of the closing of the frontier. A chronology of significant events during this period is as follows:

1803	The Louisiana Purchase is made by President Thomas Jefferson, doubling the size of the United States.
1804-1806	Jefferson sends Meriwether Lewis and William Clark on an expedition to explore the new territory; it succeeds in going to the Pacific Ocean and back.
1804-1807	Alexander Forsyth in England invents the percussion firearm ignition system.
1807	Jacob Hawken arrives in St. Louis and starts the development of the "Plains Rifle."
1812-1814	War of 1812 with England; Battle of New Orleans in January, 1815, won by riflemen under General Andrew Jackson.
1836	Colt's revolver patented in the United States; the fall of the Alamo; Texas becomes a republic; Narcissa Whitman becomes the first woman to reach the West Coast, on the Oregon Trail.
1846	War with Mexico, with Texas annexed by the United States; Colt contracts for 1,000 revolvers, which become the Dragoon Model.
1847	Colt introduces his Pocket Pistol.
1848	Sharps breechloading carbine patented.
1849	The California Gold Rush.
1851	Colt introduces the Navy Revolver.

1854	Border warfare in Kansas, with improved Sharps breech-loading carbine introduced and used.
1860	Colt New Model Army Revolver introduced.
1861	Outbreak of the Civil War; Springfield Armory's rifled musket introduced; Dr. Gatling invents a hand-cranked repeating gun.
1862	Henry rifle introduced.
1865	End of the Civil War; Springfield muskets converted to trapdoor.
1866	First Winchester rifle introduced.
1867	Cattle shipping point established at Abilene, Kansas.
1868	Union Pacific and Central Pacific Railroads meet at Promontory Point, Utah, completing the first transcontinental railroad.
1873	New Winchester rifle and the Colt Peacemaker revolver introduced.
1876	Custer and his cavalry command annihilated at the Little Bighorn.
1881	Gunfight at the O.K. Corral; Billy the Kid murdered.
1882	Formation of Buffalo Bill's Wild West show.
1890	Defeat of Native Americans at Wounded Knee; the Census declares the Frontier officially closed.

Colt and Winchester are emphasized in this chronology because they pioneered and patented two of the great advances made in firearms technology during this period, the revolver and the lever action rifle. Before that, however, the invention of the percussion cap system of ignition as against the earlier flintlock produced a large majority of the firearms used in the Civil War and for a considerable time afterward. Dr. Gatling's invention is included since it led to the modern machine gun; it could have been made available for the Civil War, and was perfected in the Custer era, when it might have saved the "Last Stand."

Special appreciation is expressed for the Buffalo Bill Historical Center and the Gene Autry Western Heritage Museum for providing most of the arms shown in this book, including many actually owned by famous historic figures of the West. The location of the former in Cody, Wyoming, is a fitting memorial to "Buffalo Bill" Cody; it includes the entire Winchester Company firearms collection, which was saved when the company's main base of operations moved from New Haven, Connecticut. The Gene Autry Museum is a stunning repository of Western memorabilia started by that prominent Western movie star in Los Angeles, supplemented by the outstanding Western, TV, and movie star collection assembled by John Bianchi. There are other notable collections of Western memorabilia, such as the National Firearms Museum referred to in the Preface, the National Cowboy and Western Heritage Museum in Oklahoma City, and the Philip R. Phillips collection at the Woolaroc Museum in Bartlesville, Oklahoma. Readers are encouraged to visit all these fine collections.

Dean K. Boorman,
New Jersey

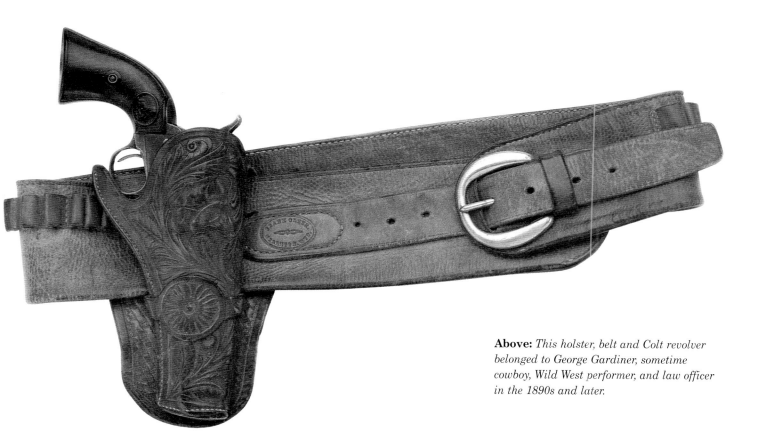

Above: *This holster, belt and Colt revolver belonged to George Gardiner, sometime cowboy, Wild West performer, and law officer in the 1890s and later.*

THE EXPLORERS

The firearms of the early explorers were flintlocks, using a system of ignition in which a piece of flint held by an exterior hammer struck a steel "frizzen," throwing sparks into a flashpan with priming powder, which in turn, through the "touch hole," set off the main charge of powder at the base or "breech" of the barrel. The gun was loaded by placing the priming powder in the flashpan, pouring the main charge of powder though the front or muzzle of the barrel, and then ramming in the bullet or, for a shotgun, a charge of shot pellets. The flintlock system came into use as early as the middle 1600s and its use continued until the middle 1800s after the percussion system was developed.

The best known single gun of the early explorers was the Model 1803 Harpers Ferry military rifle which was reputedly issued to the Lewis and Clark expedition, although this has now been disproved. Almost as famous is the compressed air rifle by Jacob Kunz of Philadelphia which accompanied the expedition, with the advantage of being able to shoot game animals without disturbing others nearby, but this was too expensive for the expedition to have had more than one. The Harpers Ferry rifle had features of the "Kentucky" rifle developed by Pennsylvania gunsmiths in the middle 1700s, evolving from the shorter, stockier German Jaeger rifle. The Kentucky rifle was carried by

early frontiersmen such as Daniel Boone, and was helpful as an auxiliary weapon in a number of Revolutionary War battles (the standard military longarm was the heavy smoothbore musket, which was faster to load and could also carry a bayonet).

The early explorers also used commercial muskets and shotguns, many of which were imported from England and were also used for trading with the Native Americans. Flintlock pistols were sometimes used for defense and for limited hunting purposes; the gunsmiths producing Kentucky rifles also made a small number of similarly designed pistols, with typical and attractive curly maple stocks.

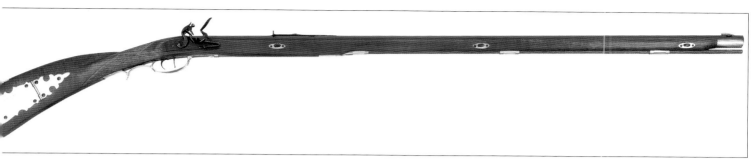

Above: *Typical Kentucky rifle, although it is a modern reproduction actually made by the Palmetto Armory in Italy. Features include an unusually long barrel with long bore, the use of striped curly maple for the stock, and brass mountings including a decorated patch box with a folding lid, at the butt end. There are double set triggers, one to prepare for firing and the other "hair" trigger requiring only a light touch for actual firing.*

KEY:

1. *Hudson's Bay multicolored four point trade blanket.*
2. *Beaver pelt of type traded by Indians to early explorers.*
3. *Iron-bound leather trunk decorated with red and blue trade cloth.*
4. *English-manufactured flintlock trade musket, about .50 caliber.*
5. *Various beads used as trade items: includes multi-colored chevron beads; amber; bone hair pipes; wire-wound beads; assorted glass beads, mostly Venetian 1700/1800.*
6. *Odometer with tin container used to measure distances on the march.*
7. *Leather case for above.*
8. *Single-breasted tanned buckskin coat with fringed cuffs and cape, fur collar, bone buttons.*
9. *Flintlock swivel-barrel rifle, maker unknown, about 1820-30, brass mounted with plain brass patch box, .45 caliber.*
10. *Powder horn carved in geometric design with carved neck.*
11. *Post ledger of Fort Bridger, Utah Terr., written by Judge W. A. Carter, 1858.*
12. *Journal of the Yellowstone Expedition, written by William Raynolds.*
13. *Wrought iron trade axe head and strike-a-light.*
14. *Sketchbook of Henry Lewis illustrating voyage on the Mississippi River by Fort Snelling, MN, to Eagle Bluffs, Northwest Terr., 1848.*
15. *MS field map, ink on line, drawn by Samuel B. Reed, chief engineer of the U.P. Railroad, depicting South Pass to the Great Salt Lake, Wyoming and Utah Terrs, 1864-65.*
16. *Harpers Ferry Model 1803 flintlock rifle, .54 caliber, one of the very few extant specimens dated 1803, the type of longarm mistakenly attributed to the Lewis and Clark expedition.*
17. *Powder horn with turned wood plus and carved neck.*
18. *Air rifle made by Jacob Kunz of Philadelphia. (Air reservoir contained in hollow metal butt; the false flint cock actuated the release of air, firing the arm.) This type of firearm was taken on the Lewis and Clark expedition.*

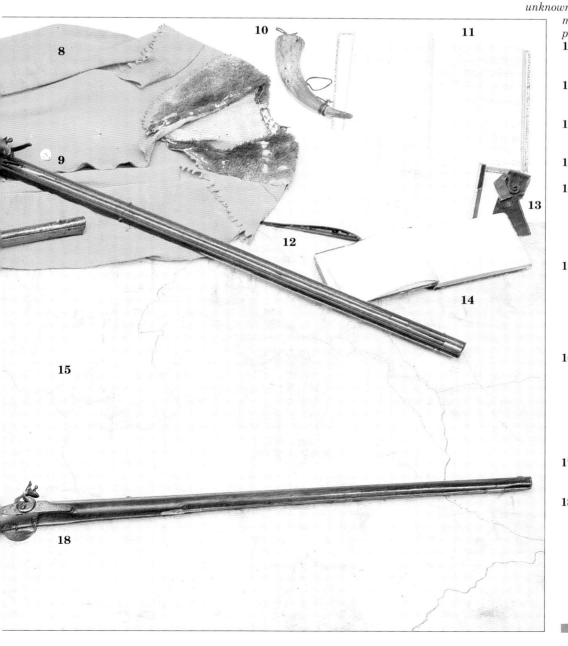

HUNTERS AND TRAPPERS

The first Americans to take advantage of the natural resources of the huge area from the Mississippi River to the Rocky Mountains added by the Louisiana Purchase of 1803 were trappers out for beaver, whose pelts were highly valued in the East and Europe. Like the French and English in Canada, the Americans began by trading with the Indians for furs but then realized they could obtain the beaver directly by trapping. Informal companies were formed in which individual trappers could bring and market their catch in a "rendezvous" held each summer. The supply of beavers, and the demand for beaver hats, both gave out before 1850, ending this early pioneering era of what

became known as "mountain men."

St. Louis, Missouri, was a major jumping-off point for trappers and others starting off into the Great Plains and the Rocky Mountains, and became a major center for assembling and manufacturing their firearms. Jacob Hawken, whose

father is thought to have worked for some time at the Harpers Ferry Arsenal, arrived in St. Louis in 1807 and opened his own gun shop in 1815. He was joined by his brother Samuel in 1822, and their Hawken "Plains" rifle became the most widely known and used on the frontier until

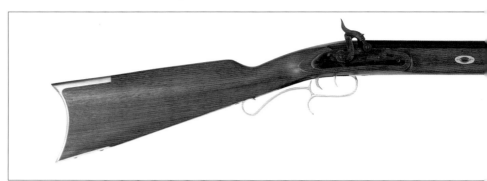

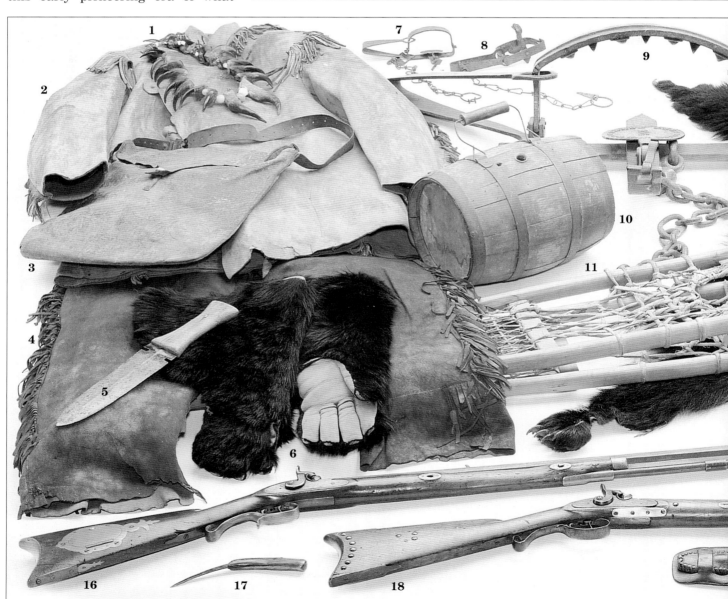

Jacob's death in 1849. It differed significantly from the Kentucky rifle in

Below: *Modern reproduction of a "Hawken Plains rifle," made by Ardesa of Spain. The heavy barrel may be noted, with plain wood for the stock and no patch box. The double set trigger is used for accuracy, as in the Kentucky rifle. Overall length is 49.0 inches, and barrel length 32.0 inches.*

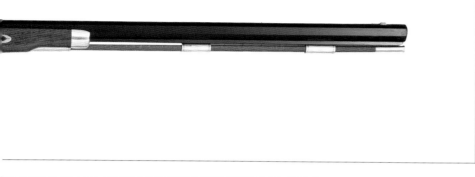

having a larger bore, suitable for Western game up to and including the buffalo. The barrel was shortened to allow use in heavy brush, and the stock was strengthened and shortened to half the length of the barrel. Some of the Hawken guns were actually smoothbores, to allow for fast loading with bullets without cloth patches wrapped around them as

was necessary for rifles.

With the advent of the percussion system of ignition, in which a copper percussion cap with fulminate ignited by the hammer took the place of the flint and flashpan, the Hawken guns became easier and more reliable to operate. Their example was followed belatedly by the military, which did not adopt the percussion system until 1841. Most earlier flintlock guns were converted to percussion by that time by the simple expedient of modifying the hammer and replacing the flashpan with a tube extending into the base of the barrel, with a nipple on the outside for the percussion cap.

Handguns similarly evolved from flintlock to percussion, still single-shot muzzleloaders until Samuel Colt's development of the revolver starting in 1836. Colt's revolver still loaded from the front, but had a cylinder holding multiple loads, providing up to six shots without reloading.

KEY:
1. *Bear claw necklace.*
2. *Heavy buckskin single-breasted coat with fringed neck, chest and sleeve ornamentation.*
3. *Leather haversack.*
4. *Elk skin leggings with fringed leg decoration.*
5. *Spear point side knife with shaped wooden hilt.*
6. *Pair of lined bearskin gloves.*
7, 8. *Metal traps with anchor chain, for small game.*
9. *Large metal bear trap.*
10. *Iron bound whiskey barrel, with handle.*
11. *Ash frame snowshoes.*
12. *Metal trap with anchor chain, for small game.*
13. *Tanned black bear skin.*
14. *Metal trap with anchor chain, for trapping medium size game.*
15. *U.S. North Model 1819 single-shot pistol, altered to percussion.*
16. *Brass-mounted, half-stocked plains rifle made by Sam Hawken, St. Louis, Missouri.*
17. *Horn-handled, iron-bladed knife used for scraping hides.*
18. *Iron-mounted, half-stocked plains rifle by Sam Hawken, with brass tack decoration.*
19. *Utility knife with double loop leather sheath and brass stud decoration.*
20. *Powder horn with carved spout and wooden plug, with iron staple for shoulder strap.*
21. *Brass double cavity bullet mold.*
22. *Iron single cavity scissors bullet mold.*

THE GUNMAKER'S SHOP

Gunmaking up until the middle of the 1800s was basically a handicraft operation. There was some specialization of labor, in which an individual had a particular specialty such as lock making, barrel forging, stock making or gun fitting. The master of the shop would do the final fitting assembly; a part from one gun could rarely be used in another since it would not have the same dimensions. The accompanying illustration (below) is of a reconstruction of a colonial gun shop of the 1800 to 1810 era, showing the forging furnace and the tools used for a typical three- or four-man operation.

Often on the frontier obsolete or discarded military weapons were used or converted for civilian use, as shown in the illustration. The longarms on the windowsill to the right are a Model 1777 French musket such as used by the American troops during the Revolution, and a Model 1795 musket of the same pattern, produced by the Springfield and Harpers Ferry armories. A brass-mounted Kentucky rifle is shown in the corner at the left. It was in this kind of shop that the Hawkens and others started their thriving gun business in response to the need for firearms by the Western pioneers.

In 1841, in far-off Vermont, a revolution began in gunmaking which eventually extended to all of American technology. Two young entrepreneurs, Robbins and Lawrence, put in a successful bid for the production of 10,000 military rifles of an advanced pattern, which the Army realized it needed for the impending war with Mexico. Since there were few craftsmen available in the central Vermont area, Robbins and Lawrence developed machine tools such as the turret lathe and the milling machine. These could not only replace skilled craftsmen with less skilled workers, but could produce a greater output and, significantly, the guns produced had interchangeable parts, all made to the same dimen-

sions. This approach was so successful, the 10,000 being produced a year ahead of schedule, that even the English sent a special commission which bought a set of the Robbins and Lawrence machine tools for the British government's rifle factory at Enfield. Sam Colt subsequently adopted this "American System" of manufacturing, displayed his products at the Crystal Palace Exhibition in London in 1851, and then established in London a branch of his large factory in Hartford, Connecticut.

Right: *Workshop as in Colt's Hartford factory, showing his new system in which the workers were assigned separately to making individual parts, rather than craftsmen making entire firearms.*

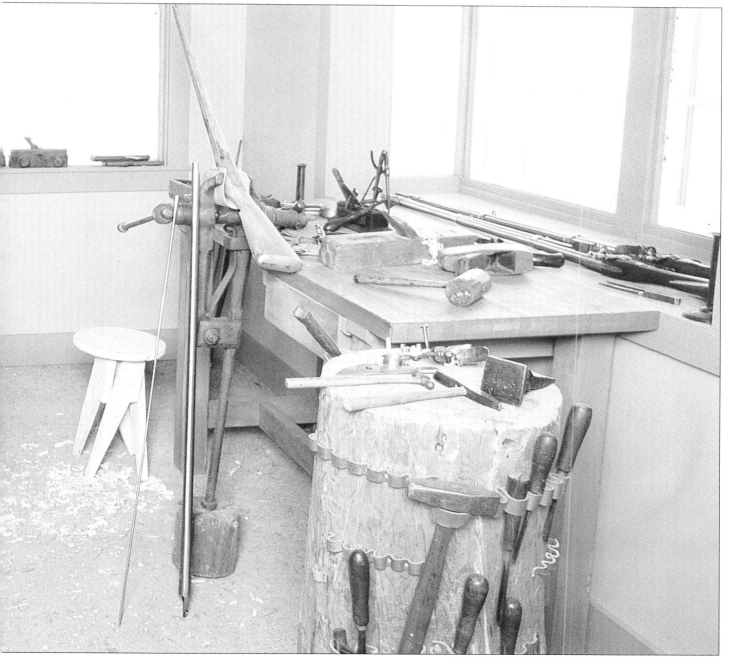

THE HANDGUN IN THE WEST AND ON THE FRONTIER

The use of handguns in the West and its expanding frontier began with the revolution – the temptation is to make a pun! – resulting from Sam Colt's revolver. Most of the handguns in the accompanying illustration, which are representative of those used in the West up to 1890, are Colts, since the company held the patent on revolvers up to 1857.

Just how revolutionary this development was can be appreciated by comparing these weapons with the single-shot muzzleloading pistol shown as item 15 among the collection of trappers' items on page 13. That was heavy, clumsy, and even when used by the military in pairs in saddle holsters, could not produce more than two shots at a time.

The following description by Angus Laidlaw, a contributing editor of *American Rifleman* magazine, underlines the significance of Colt's invention and how it works, right up to the present time:

"Colt did for firearms what the Wright brothers did for the airplane; he, as they, assembled components of then-current technology into a new more practical form to accomplish what had never quite been done before. The Wrights combined the gasoline engine turning an airscrew with a three-axis control system to create the first controllable powered airplane in 1903. Between his ocean voyage in 1830 and his first U.S. Patent, No. 138, issued February 25, 1836, Sam Colt mated the percussion ignition system with mechanically unlocking, turning and relocking the cylinder by cocking the hammer. This concept made his five-shooters the first practical fast-firing repeaters when they came out of his Paterson, New Jersey, factory in 1836. Before the Wrights, there were gliders, propellers, and engines. Before Colt there were flintlock revolvers like the Collier with cylinders that had to be unlatched, turned, and relatched by hand besides pulling back the flintlock cock and operating the frizzen-cum-priming magazine. This was quicker than reloading for each shot, but not exactly rapid fire.

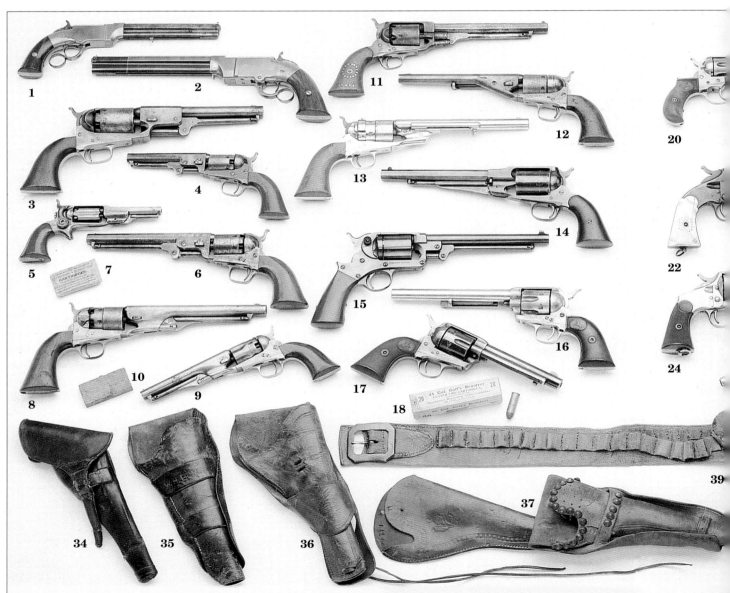

(Artifacts courtesy of Gene Autry Western Heritage Museum, Los Angeles, California.)

KEY:

1. *Volcanic lever-action No. 1 Navy pistol.*
2. *Volcanic lever-action No. 2 Navy pistol.*
3. *Colt Third Model Dragoon revolver.*
4. *Colt Model 1849 Pocket Revolver, .31 caliber.*
5. *Colt Model 1855 Sidehammer Pocket Revolver, second series.*
6. *Colt Model 1851 Navy revolver, .36 caliber.*
7. *Full pack of 6 Hazard's .36 caliber cartridges.*
8. *Colt Model 1860 Army revolver, .44 caliber.*
9. *Colt Model 1862 Police revolver, .36 caliber.*
10. *Full pack of 6 Johnson and Dow .44 caliber combustible cartridges.*
11. *Whitney second model Navy revolver, .36 cal.*
12. *Colt Model 1861 Navy revolver, factory alteration to cartridge.*
13. *Colt Model 1860 Army revolver, Richards alteration, .44 caliber.*
14. *Remington New Model Army revolver, factory alteration to cartridge.*
15. *Starr Arms Company single action Model 1863 Army revolver.*
16. *Colt Single Action Army revolver, .38-40 caliber.*
17. *Colt Single Action Army revolver, .45 caliber.*
18. *Full box of 20 rounds of .45 caliber ammunition.*
19. *Colt Single Action Army revolver, .45 caliber.*
20. *Colt Double Action Thunderer revolver.*
21. *Colt Model 1878 Double Action Army revolver.*
22. *Merwin, Hulbert and Company Army single action Model 1863 Army revolver.*
23. *Merwin, Hulbert and Company Army revolver, early model with bird's head butt.*
24. *Hopkins and Allen XL no. 8 Army revolver, .44 caliber.*
25. *Forehand & Wadsworth new model Army revolver.*
26. *Smith & Wesson Model 3 single action revolver, .44 S&W caliber.*
27. *S&W No. 2 Army revolver, .32 caliber.*
28. *S&W First Model American single action revolver, .44 S&W caliber.*
29. *S&W double action first model revolver.*
30. *Manhattan Firearms Co. pocket model revolver, .31 caliber.*
31. *Full box of 50 rounds .38 caliber Winchester centerfire ammunition and five loose rounds of .38 caliber rimfire.*
32. *Deringer pocket revolver, .32 caliber.*
33. *Colt Cloverleaf Model revolver, .41 caliber.*
34. *Gutta-Percha holster.*
35. *Double-loop holster for a Colt Single Action Army revolver.*
36. *Single-loop holster for Colt Model 1878 Double Action Army revolver.*
37. *Embossed holster for a Colt Single Action Army revolver.*
38. *Double-loop holster made from a military flap holster for a Colt Model 1861 Navy revolver, altered to cartridge, with belt.*
39. *Double-loop holster for a Colt Single Action Army revolver.*
40. *Full box of 50 rounds of .44 cal. S&W special ammunition.*
41. *Military flap holster for a percussion revolver.*
42. *Hand-made holster with rawhide seam for a Colt Single Action Army revolver.*
43. *Buckskin California or "Slim Jim" open top holster for Navy size .36 caliber revolver.*

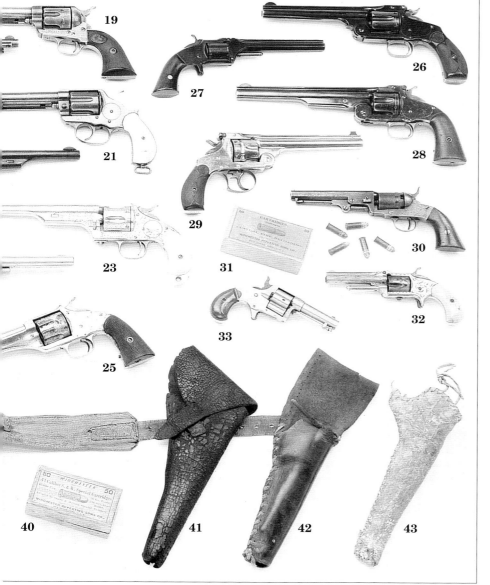
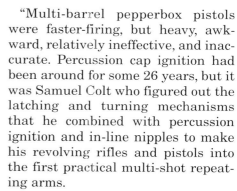

"Multi-barrel pepperbox pistols were faster-firing, but heavy, awkward, relatively ineffective, and inaccurate. Percussion cap ignition had been around for some 26 years, but it was Samuel Colt who figured out the latching and turning mechanisms that he combined with percussion ignition and in-line nipples to make his revolving rifles and pistols into the first practical multi-shot repeating arms.

"The basic concept is of having the hammer do all the work, a straightforward but far from easy proposition. The cylinder must be locked in line with the barrel when fired by caps on nipples in-line with the cylinder, a feature of his patent. It must unlock to be turned to the next chamber. Cocking the hammer must accomplish this. The hand, a spring-loaded arm pinned to the side of the hammer, engages ratchet teeth on the back of the cylinder to turn it (or a ring which in turn engages the cylinder). As cocking the hammer begins to raise the hand to start turning the cylinder, a beveled cam-stud on the other side of the hammer bears on a spring arm of a bolt in the frame below the cylinder to lower it out of the locking notch, freeing the cylinder to turn. The cylinder locks again when the hammer is fully cocked and then falls to fire the chamber.

"This basic mechanism, with varia-

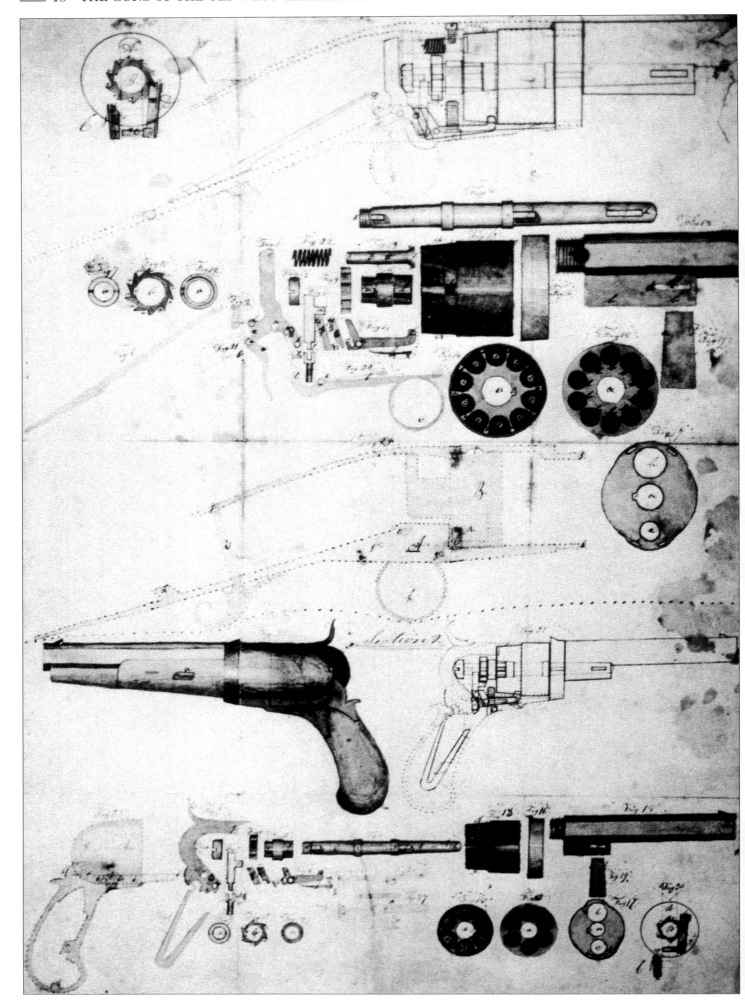

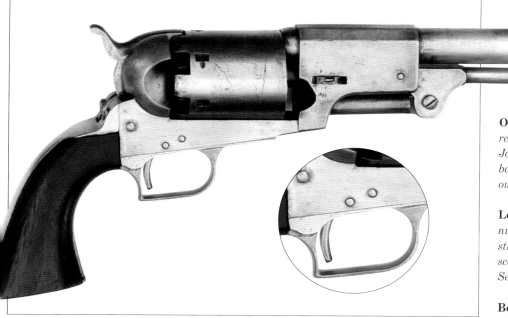

Opposite page: *Original drawings of Colt's revolver and the models made for him by John Pearson about 1834-5, which were the basis for the original American patent taken out by Colt in 1836.*

Left and inset: *Model 1859 Dragoon, serial number 5818, with 7.5in barrel. The cylinder still bears traces of a "Red Indian" combat scene. Square triggerguard shows this is the Second Model Dragoon.*

Below: *Engraved Third Model Dragoon, with characteristic rounded triggerguard, and cutaway showing the interior workings, together with a series of key parts.*

tions for double action revolvers where a long trigger pull cocks the hammer, still unlocks the cylinder, then turns and relocks it before dropping the hammer to fire in all current-production revolvers. Cartridge revolvers with Sam Colt's basic single action mechanisms are still being made by Colt's in West Hartford, Connecticut, and some of their internal parts still interchange with those of the 1851 percussion Navy Colt."

Handguns were probably popular in the West partly for the same reason that they are today among collectors and target shooters – for their mechanical interest, their attractive appearance, and because they are fun to shoot. Self-defense was important, especially in areas that were settled before the law arrived, and a revolver was handy when encountering a rattlesnake. On the other hand, they were relatively expensive, more

than a cowboy's monthly salary. In any event, some idea can be gained of the number of handguns used in the West by the more than one million revolvers Colt produced up to 1890. Many were used in the Civil War, and some were sold overseas, including to Australia where there is now an active collectors' market.

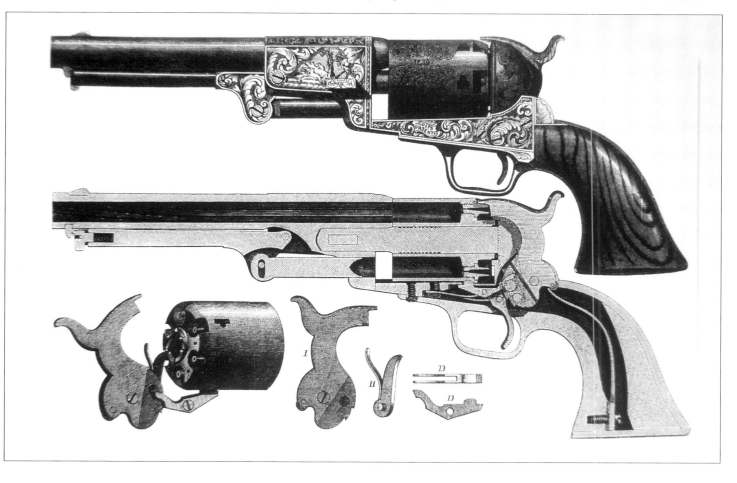

COLT PATERSON REVOLVERS

As a New Jerseyan himself, the writer is constantly surprised at how few collectors and shooters in that state know that Sam Colt began making his guns there, in the industrial city of Paterson. This was in 1836, in a four-story factory building owned by his cousin Roswell Colt. Sam was only 21 years old at the time. He had envisioned a workable

Below, left: *Colt prototype revolver with folding bayonet, made by blacksmith John Pearson about 1834-5.*

Below, right: *Five-shot, single action Holster or Texas Paterson revolver in .36in caliber, made between 1838 and 1840.*

revolver as early as age 15, supposedly inspired by the movement of the ship's wheel while working as a seaman on a sailing ship to India. A natural salesman, he traveled around the country doing shows with laughing gas as "Dr. Coult of Calcutta," while engaging gunsmiths to develop working models of his revolver. He took out patents in 1835 in England and in 1836 in the United States, giving him a monopoly on the new invention all the way up to 1857.

The factory in Paterson operated until 1842, and produced 1,912 revolving rifles and shotguns as well as 2,850 revolving pistols. While the guns were beautifully designed and

crafted, the enterprise was not a commercial success. Colt was inexperienced in running a business, the guns were expensive, complicated, and fragile (a pistol blew up at an Army trial), and the dirty black powder available at the time would foul the arms' delicate mechanisms. Colt was correct at the time in thinking that it was longarms that would be the most useful in the West, but ulti-

Above: *Texas Model Paterson, with loading lever applied, of the Ehler period production. This example was carried by Jorge Rivas, a scout for the Confederate Army during the Civil War.*

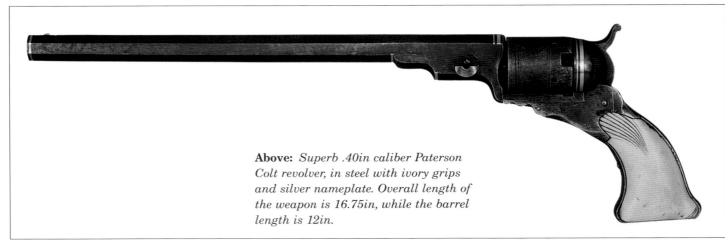

Above: *Superb .40in caliber Paterson Colt revolver, in steel with ivory grips and silver nameplate. Overall length of the weapon is 16.75in, while the barrel length is 12in.*

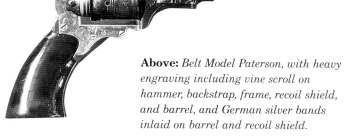

Above: *Belt Model Paterson, with heavy engraving including vine scroll on hammer, backstrap, frame, recoil shield, and barrel, and German silver bands inlaid on barrel and recoil shield.*

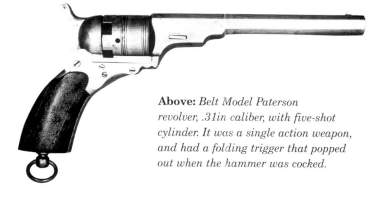

Above: *Belt Model Paterson revolver, .31in caliber, with five-shot cylinder. It was a single action weapon, and had a folding trigger that popped out when the hammer was cocked.*

mately the idea of the revolver was really only practical for handguns.

The Paterson experience was invaluable for Colt both in having his patent established and in laying the groundwork for his later success. What is now the State of Texas seceded from Mexico and declared itself a separate republic in the very year, 1836, in which Colt established his Paterson factory. Anxious to try any new invention to bolster its defenses against hostile Native Americans as well as the Mexicans, the new republic purchased 180 Paterson Holster pistols and 280 rifles and carbines. These were used with considerable success, for example in "Hays' Big Fight," in which fifteen Texas Rangers defeated some eighty Comanche Indians, who mistakenly thought the Rangers had single-shot guns that would take time to reload while the braves attacked.

The Paterson pistols were made in three calibers: .28in, the Pocket Model or "Baby Paterson"; .31in, the Belt Model; and .36in, the Holster Model, also known as the Texas Paterson. Historian R. L. Wilson was shown on television's History Channel successfully firing one of these rare arms, and commenting on the watch-like precision of its mechanism. Values on the collectors' market run to over $150,000.

Above: *Colt Paterson longarms. Top one is a Model 1839 revolving shotgun in .61in caliber smoothbore. Lower one is a First Model Ring Lever revolving rifle made in 1837; calibers were .34 to .44in.*

Left: *Cased Paterson Belt Model revolver with accessories, about 1838-40.*

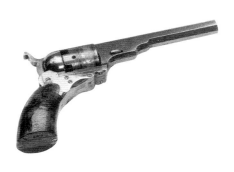

PERCUSSION COLTS FROM HARTFORD

Sam Colt was able to establish a new factory in Hartford, Connecticut, where the company is still located today, as a result of the Texans' appreciation of his revolver. After Texas was admitted to the Union in 1846 and the Mexican War began, Captain Samuel Walker, a former Texas Ranger, came to Washington D.C. and corresponded with Sam Colt about designing a new military handgun, subsequently known as the Walker Dragoon. The Army Ordnance Department issued a contract for 1,000 of these pistols. Having no factory of his own, Colt had the guns made by the Eli Whitney Company in New Haven, Connecticut, and used the proceeds, along with some of the Whitney machinery, to set up his own factory in Hartford. He engaged Elisha King Root as his plant superintendent, and Root designed and patented an integrated system of special purpose machines, following the "American System" of manufacturing pioneered by Robbins and Lawrence.

The Walker Model continued basically unchanged as the Colt Dragoon in three models up to 1861. In .44in caliber and a massive 4 pounds 9 ounces in weight, it was a powerful weapon designed especially for use on horseback with pommel holsters. It had an engraved scene on the cylinder, appropriately enough, of early U.S. Cavalrymen known as "Dragoons" battling against a group of Native American horsemen. The Dragoon was also assembled and sold at Colt's London factory, which opened from 1853 to 1857, after Colt guns were featured in the 1851 Crystal Palace Exhibition.

Colt began to produce a .31in caliber pocket revolver in 1848, called the Baby Dragoon, but came out with an updated version the following year, called the Model 1849 Pocket. This was the year that gold was discovered at Sutter's Mill in California, and it was undoubtedly the Gold Rush that followed which spurred the demand for this popular handgun. The balance in firearms shifted from hunting, trapping, and defense

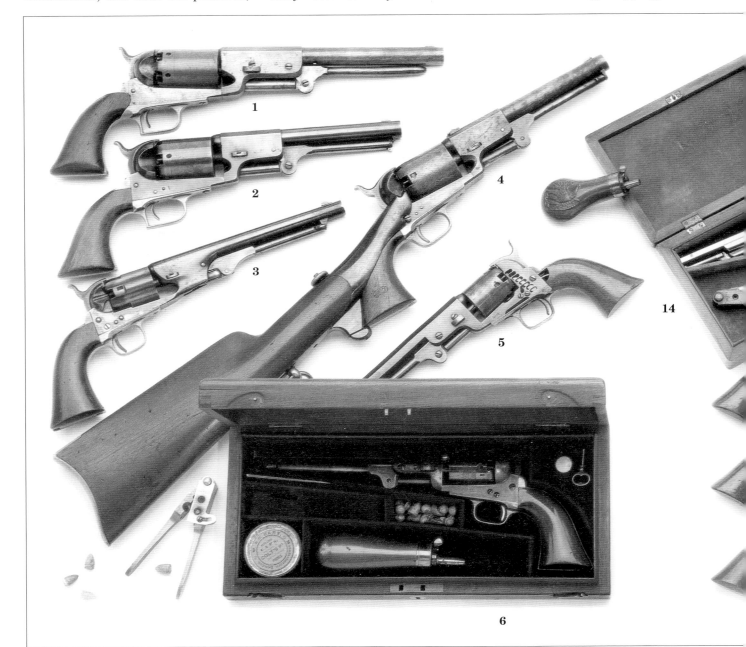

(Artifacts courtesy of Gene Autry Western Heritage Museum, Los Angeles, California.)

against Native Americans and Mexicans to self-defense in situations where the law was not effective.

Total production of this attractive model up to 1873 was about 325,000. Its interesting cylinder scene is a bit of Colt advertising: a stagecoach driver in the process of shooting six (the number of shots in the cylinder) would-be robbers.

A second highly popular percussion revolver was bought out two years after the Pocket Model, the Model 1851 Navy Revolver, in .36in caliber. In several variations up to 1873, its production was about 315,000. Neither the Pocket Model nor the Navy Model was issued in quantity by the Army, but many were purchased by officers and others in the Civil War, in addition to being used in the West.

The cylinder scene for the Navy was a battle between sailing and paddlewheel ships of the Texas and Mexican Navies. The same scene was used for the Model 1861 Army in .44in caliber. The terms are misleading: "Navy" is separated from "Army" only to distinguish the different calibers, not to indicate that there was any difference in their use by the two services.

The Model 1861 Army was introduced at the beginning of the Civil War, and was adopted by the military as standard issue; civilian-marked 1861 Armys are rare. Its production totaled about 200,500.

Sam Colt himself did not live to see the end of production of his percussion pistols. He died shortly after the start of the Civil War, in January 1862. His wife continued the expansion of the business, however, even though set back by a disastrous fire in February, 1864, which destroyed most of the factory; the company and the factory went on to new heights after the later introduction of cartridge arms.

The design of Colt's percussion pistols made a detour in 1855 with the .28in and .31in caliber "Root Models," with a solid frame and side hammer. These were complicated but fairly popular, with total production about 40,000.

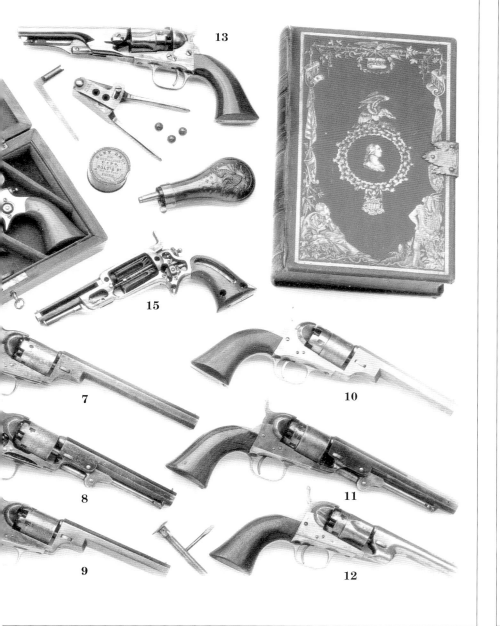

KEY:
1. *The massive Walker model revolver, .44 caliber, popular in the Mexican War. One of 100 civilian models that were made after the completion of the 1847 government contract.*
2. *First Model Dragoon revolver, .44 caliber, made in 1848.*
3. *Model 1860 Colt Army revolver, .44 caliber, experimental model, serial number 4, with fluted cylinder. Thousands saw use in the hands of civilians and Western cavalry in the 1860s and early 1870s.*
4. *Third Model Dragoon revolver, with attachable shoulder stock, .44 caliber, carried by dragoon and cavalry troops in the pre-Civil War West.*
5. *1851 Navy Model, .36 caliber, cutaway demonstration model.*
6. *Cased 1851 Navy, with London markings.*
7. *Model 1848 pocket revolver, known as the "Baby Dragoon," lightweight, easy to carry, and popular throughout the West.*
8. *Model 1849 Pocket Revolver, .31 caliber, five-shot, cutaway demonstrator made in 1857.*
9. *Prototype of the "Wells Fargo" Model 1849 Pocket Revolver, serial number 1, in .31 caliber, with separate loading tool – easily concealed, but all business.*
10. *Experimental pocket revolver, unfinished, in .36 caliber.*
11. *Model 1862 Pocket Navy revolver, made in 1863, stagecoach hold-up scene engraved on the cylinder.*
12. *"Trapper's" Model 1862 Police revolver, experimental prototype, without serial number.*
13. *Model 1862 Police revolver with accessories, inscribed "H. A. Bridham / U.S.A." with rare casing in the form of a book.*
14. *Cased Model 1855 sidehammer revolver with accessories, caliber .28, made in about 1856, the cylinder roll engraved with a scene of an Indian fight.*
15. *Standard Model 1856 sidehammer revolver, cutaway demonstrator.*

SINGLE AND DOUBLE ACTION REVOLVERS

It was not until 1877, long after Sam Colt's death in 1862, that his company produced a double action revolver. "Double action" means that instead of having to cock the hammer by hand as with a single action pistol, the shooter can cock the hammer with a hard pull on the trigger.

Some double action revolvers can also be used in the single action mode, and others can be fired only double action.

Mechanically, there is not a great deal of difference between single and double action. With the latter, a strut is added between the trigger and the hammer to connect the trigger movement to the hammer. At the top of the cycle, the top of the trigger slips beyond the strut so that the hammer is released, or so that if the hammer is pulled back manually, it will stay in a full cock position until the trigger is pulled.

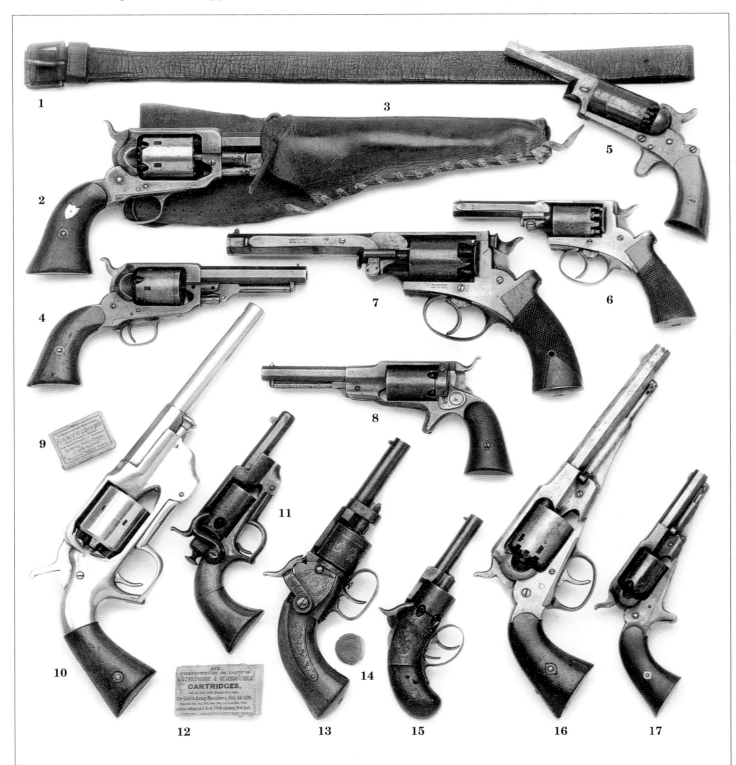

(Artifacts courtesy of Buffalo Bill Historical Center, Cody, Wyoming.)

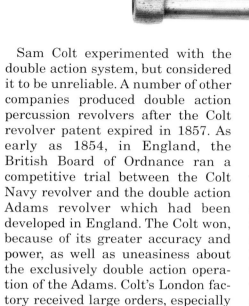

Sam Colt experimented with the double action system, but considered it to be unreliable. A number of other companies produced double action percussion revolvers after the Colt revolver patent expired in 1857. As early as 1854, in England, the British Board of Ordnance ran a competitive trial between the Colt Navy revolver and the double action Adams revolver which had been developed in England. The Colt won, because of its greater accuracy and power, as well as uneasiness about the exclusively double action operation of the Adams. Colt's London factory received large orders, especially from the British Navy. However, in 1855, the Adams was modified by the Beaumont patent so that it could be used either single- or double action, and at that point, probably partly to spite the Americans, the British Board of Ordnance changed permanently to the Adams design (see accompanying illustration for the Adams as made in the United States.)

Firing a pistol in the double action mode is obviously faster, since only one hand or motion is needed, but it is less accurate because the trigger pull is harder and the instant of discharge more difficult to gauge. It is noteworthy that the modern 9mm caliber automatic pistols now carried by most police departments are double action on the first shot, meaning that there is no delay in cocking the gun, with the recoil action doing the cocking for each successive shot.

Especially with later cartridge pistols like the Colt Single Action Army, techniques were developed to make single action shooting faster. One method was "fanning," in which the shooter used rapid movements of the heel of the hand used for cocking, while the trigger was held down by the other hand or taped down or completely removed. A second method was "slip" shooting, in which the gun was held with one hand and aimed, while the hammer was worked rapidly with the thumb of the other hand by pressing or flipping it back to full cock position and letting it "slip" from under the thumb. However, the famous exhibition shooter Ed McGivern, in his 1938 book *Fast and Fancy Revolver Shooting*, states that after extensive tests he determined that single action shooting cannot be as fast as double action.

McGivern's tests were indeed extensive. In an article in American Rifleman magazine in October 1932 he recounts his findings of tests with a Colt Single Action Army "with no more special work done on it than any frontiersman could have obtained from a good gunsmith." He reports that, as recorded by accurate electric and photographic timing

Above: *Used by the Confederates during the Civil War, the French-designed Le Mat revolver was deadly. Immediately beneath the main barrel sat an 18-gauge shotgun barrel on which the cylinder revolved. When the nine loads in the cylinder were expended, an adjustment of the hammer brought the scatter load to bear.*

devices, only one-fourth to three-fifths of a second were required for drawing and shooting one shot into a man-sized mark at ten yards. With fanning or slip shooting, using two hands for one gun, five shots into a target covered by a man's hand were delivered at ten yards in one-and-one-fifth seconds. One has to bear in mind that these tests were undertaken by one of the world's greatest firearms practitioners. The conclusion is that some of the men in the West whose lives had depended for years on their ability to shoot quickly and straight would have done nearly as well. However, Hollywood's depiction of fast and accurate hand-

KEY:
1. Belts varied in width; some were plain, but by the mid-1870s cartridge loops were common. Before then most people carried saddle bags or ammunition pouches.
2. .36 caliber Whitney Navy pistol (s.n. 14457) that rivaled both Colt and Remington; well made and popular.
3. The pistol's original holster.
4. Whitney five-shot .31 caliber pocket model. On both the Navy and Pocket pistols, the cylinder pin was attached to the rammer and held in place by a pin through the frame.
5. The Walch ten-shot .31 pocket pistol.
6. Massachusetts Arms Co.'s licensed copy of the British Beaumont-Adams .31 pocket pistol.
7. The MAC's version of the Beaumont-Adams Army Model in .44
8. Remington-Beals Army pocket revolver.
9. Box of .31 caliber combustible cartridges.
10. Allen & Wheelock's center hammer Army revolver in .44 caliber.
11. Allen & Wheelock's center hammer pocket revolver in .28 caliber.
12. Six .44 caliber combustible cartridges for the Colt 1860 Army revolver.
13. MAC's Maynard primed belt revolver, .31 caliber.
14. Maynard's cap primers.
15. Springfield Arms Co. pocket revolver in .28 caliber.
16. Remington-Rider double action New Model belt revolver (1863) in .36 caliber.
17. Remington New Model pocket revolver (1863) in .31 caliber.

caliber. A number of these were purchased by the Confederacy.

gun shooting at more than ten yards has to be regarded with some skepticism. As recounted elsewhere, the actual gunfight romanticized so entertainingly by movie makers in The Gunfight at the OK Corral, in Tombstone, Arizona, was fought at close range, largely with revolvers, and with no great accuracy.

After Colt's patent on the revolver mechanism expired in 1857, there was a proliferation of copies and modifications, as shown in the accompanying illustrations. Most of these firearms were of the simpler single action design, which may be partly accounted for because of the

Above: *A Massachusetts Arms Company Adams-patent Navy revolver, actually a British design produced under license in the United States.*

British Adams patent on its double action mechanism. British officers liked fast-shooting arms for use at close quarters, but their heavy trigger pull naturally affected accuracy at longer ranges. The Beaumont-Adams lock overcame this disadvantage by giving the firer a choice of single action or self-cocking.

A competitor for Colt's was Remington, which developed a series of percussion revolvers starting in 1857 and culminating with the New Model Army in .44in caliber. Approximately 122,000 of this model were produced, and it was one of the major handguns used during the Civil War. Interestingly, the Remington-Rider Pocket Revolver of 1860 to 1873 was a double action model, and some of the later production were converted to the .32in rimfire cartridge developed by Smith & Wesson, and thus became the first American double action cartridge revolvers.

The Le Mat revolver, as shown, with ten shots in the cylinder plus a central shotgun barrel, was certainly the most ambitious adaptation of the percussion revolver system. Made primarily in Europe, a number of these were used by Confederate forces in the Civil War. The revolver was patented in the United States by

Jean Alexander Le Mat in 1856. It was of massive and solid construction. The frame, including the butt, was made in one piece, the lower barrel being an integral part of it. The cylinder was mounted on this lower barrel, which thus doubled as an axis pin. The upper barrel was mounted on the lower one by means of a front and rear ring, the latter having an extension which locked firmly on to the lower part of the frame. The lower barrel, which was smoothbored, was of cylindrical shape; the upper barrel, which was rifled, was octagonal and was fitted with a foresight. The weapon's rearsight was an integral part of the hammer nose (unfortunately missing in the specimen in the photo).

The awkward appearing but rugged Allen & Wheelock .44in mili-

Above: *The Beaumont-Adams five-shot .49in caliber Dragoon revolver: overall length, 13in; barrel, 7in; weight 47 ounces. Its double action lock was invented by Lt. F. Beaumont of Britain's Royal Engineers. A rammer was also fitted, whose lever was held against the barrel by light spring pressure against a stud, and when the lever was drawn upwards, the rammer itself was thrust backward with considerable force.*

tary revolver, as well as the Pettengill and the similar but more successful Savage, also saw service in the Civil War.

However, most of the percussion revolvers were closely modeled on the Colt. A system that was an attempt to avoid the need for putting on separate percussion caps was the Maynard tape primer system, which worked similarly to a toy cap pistol.

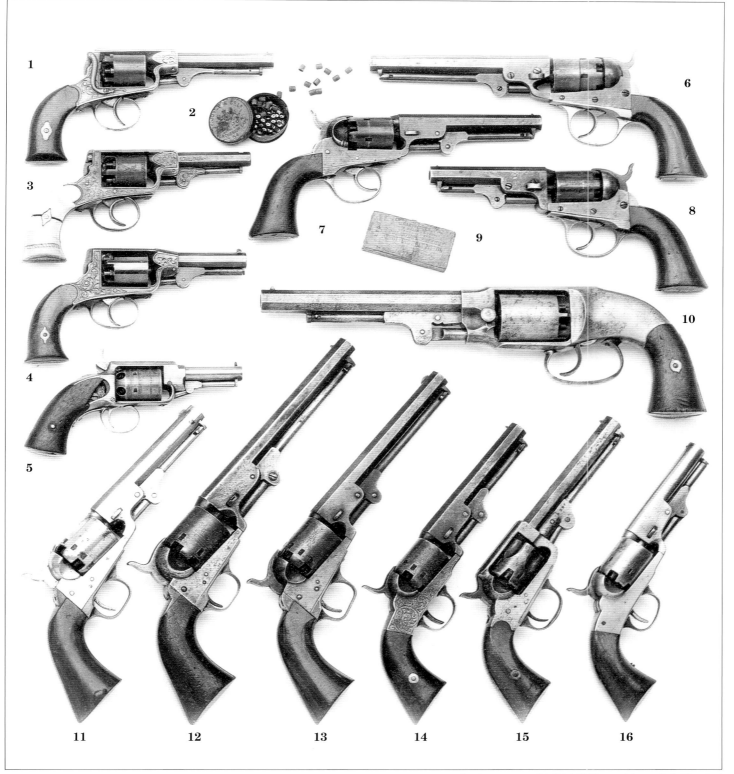

(Artifacts courtesy of Buffalo Bill Historical Center, Cody, Wyoming.)

KEY:

1. *IXL revolver believed made before 1857, based upon the British Adams.*
2. *Box of British-made Joyce percussion caps.*
3. *Another version of the IXL revolver; B. J. Hart of New York is often credited with manufacture.*
4. *Another version of the IXL.*
5. *James Warner revolver.*
6. *Cooper double action Navy revolver with a rebated cylinder; .36 caliber, five-shot.*
7. *Cooper five-shot .31 double action pocket pistol.*
8. *Cooper pocket model; note close resemblance to Colt's pistols.*
9. *Package of combustible pistol cartridges. Sold in packs of six but larger quantities were available. Most civilians also had reserves of loose powder, ball and caps.*
10. *Pettengill's double action hammerless Army pistol: six-shot, .44 caliber.*
11. *Manhattan's five-shot .36 caliber "Navy" pistol that some confused with Colt's pistols.*
12. *Metropolitan Arms Co.'s copy of Colt's 1861 Navy.*
13. *Manhattan 6-inch barreled Navy pistol.*
14. *Manhattan .31 caliber five-shot pocket pistol.*
15. *Union Arms Company pocket pistol with fluted cylinder.*
16. *Hopkins & Allen pocket pistol.*

DERINGERS 1845-1860

Colt's monopoly on the revolver did not prevent other manufacturers from developing single-shot pistols which would be useful in the West. A popular type was the "hide-out" short, concealable pistol known to be favored by gamblers, gunfighters, or indeed anyone who feared being caught unawares. The best-known type was introduced by Henry Deringer, a Philadelphia rifle maker, in the early 1840s: a single-shot percussion pistol of large caliber, typically .41in, less than six inches in length. This class of pistol is also referred to as the "Derringer,"

one explanation being that when one was used by John Wilkes Booth in 1865 to assassinate President Abraham Lincoln, the extra "r" crept into a reporter's story. However, when Charles Cora killed General William Richardson with a Deringer pistol in San Francisco in 1855, a lawless time where committees of vigilantes were prevalent, newspaper accounts used the double "r."

Deringers were attractively mounted and decorated, as shown in the accompanying illustrations. Their length varied down to a miniature size fitting in the palm of a

hand. Most did not have ramrods, which apparently was not a problem since any implement could be used to seat the bullet. There were rudimentary sights, but the pistols were ordinarily used at point blank range.

The Deringer was so popular that there were a number of imitators, such as Slotter, who had worked for Henry Deringer. Also, it is reported that a Philadelphia tailor named Jacob Deringer allowed, for a fee, the use of his name, as J. Deringer, to be put on other gunmakers' pistols.

Among other small pistols competing with the Deringer, that of the

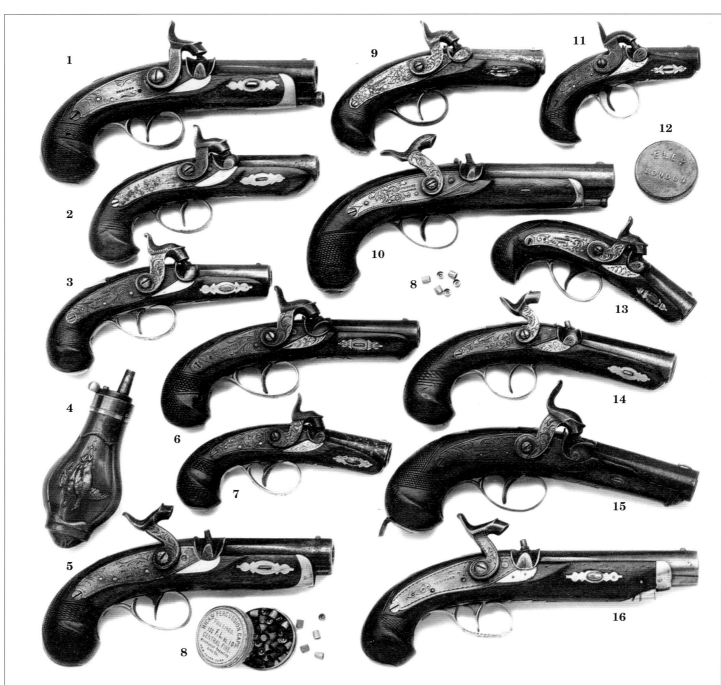

(Artifacts courtesy of Buffalo Bill Historical Center, Cody, Wyoming.)

Ethan Allen Company in Massachusetts used a bar hammer system instead of the traditional sidelock. Allen was mainly known for pepperboxes, which also used a bar hammer coming down on the top of the barrel, but joined five or six barrels rotating around a central axis. Each barrel

KEY:
1. *A version of the Allen bar hammer pistol.*
2. *A Blunt & Syms sidehammer pocket pistol*
3. *Bacon & Co. single-shot ring trigger pistol.*
4. *Massachusetts Arms Co. single-shot pocket pistol fitted with Maynard's tape primer mechanism.*
5. *Lindsay two-shot belt pistol.*
6. *Unmarked .28 caliber single-shot breechloading pocket pistol.*

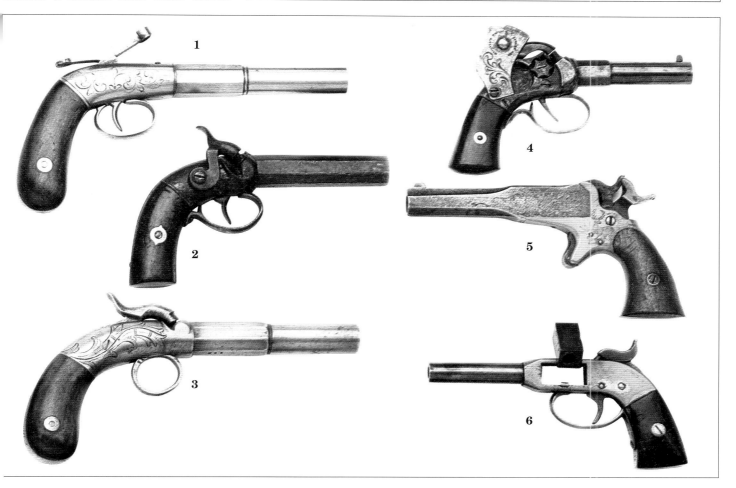

KEY:
1. *Henry Deringer's pocket pistols were the best of their day. This is the medium size pocket pistol with ramrod.*
2. *Deringer small size pistol; German silver was used for triggerguards and as stock decoration.*
4. *Typical powder flask.*
5. *The percussion lock was a boon to Deringer and others.*
6. *Deringer's pistols all followed the same graceful lines. Smaller ones, however, could be hidden in the palm of a hand.*
7. *Engraving on Deringer pistols was mostly confined to the lock plate.*
8. *A tin of American-made percussion caps.*
9. *A small size pistol – compare the sizes.*
10. *A medium size pistol complete with ramrod.*
11. *"Baby" of the family, and probably the most famous version. John Wilkes Booth used one of these in .41 caliber to kill Lincoln.*
12. *Eley Brothers of London supplied millions of percussion caps to American makers (Colt notably).*
13. *Although clearly marked, Deringer's pistols were widely copied, some even bearing his name.*
14. *The sights on a Deringer were basic, and consisted of a blade front sight and a "V" cut into a plate behind the nipple housing. Most users ignored the sights and fired point-blank*
15. *Checkering was common to most Deringer stocks.*
16. *A handsome pistol of the larger size minus its ramrod.*

had a nipple with a percussion cap at its base and a trigger operated by double action, meaning that pulling the trigger cocked and released the hammer. A ratchet would turn the multiple barrels around their central axis after each shot. Like the single-shot bar hammer pistols, this system was not adaptable to larger calibers like the Colt or the Deringer, but nevertheless achieved considerable popularity.

Among other short, concealable pistols, a number of English flintlock "muff pistols" were converted to percussion, and an attempt was made by one manufacturer to use the Maynard tape priming system as referred to on page 26. This used a roll of tape with primers attached, as in a toy cap pistol. As was the case with longarms, however, this system was unreliable and not widely used.

DERINGERS 1860 AND AFTER

If Sam Colt's invention of the repeating pistol was a revolution in handguns, another was the invention of the self-contained cartridge, complete with a primer set off by the firing pin, a case of copper or brass, and the bullet at the front of the case seated on a charge of gunpowder. Daniel Wesson, in partnership with Horace Smith in a predecessor to the Winchester Repeating Arms Company, patented a .22in rimfire cartridge in 1854. This was after experimenting with the more primitive French Flobert cartridge.

When the .22in cartridge became widely available in 1859 (Oliver Winchester perfected the .44in cartridge in 1860 for his Henry rifle), there was a new proliferation of Deringer-type pistols. In saloons, gambling houses, and bordellos, men concealed these pistols in boot tops, sleeve cuffs, waistbands, or even inside hats. These pistols were also popular with ladies, of whom the well-bred tended to carry them in their handbags, while those of uncertain virtue hid them in their stocking tops or even, occasionally, in the form of a garter or "crotch pouch!"

The first shot from a Deringer might not always have achieved the desired result, giving rise to the need for a multi-shot weapon such as two, three- or even four-barreled versions, and at least one gun had a bayonet attachment. The weapons had minimal range, but were deadly close-in, such as in a crowded saloon or across a card table.

Several gunsmiths apart from Deringer made pocket pistols, among them Ethan Allen, American Arms Co., Eben T. Starr, and most famously Remington and Colt, the most prolific producer; and, as usual, some of these were highly decorated. The type was largely superseded by the "Suicide Special" small revolvers of the 1890s, and then by small semi-automatic pistols.

KEY:
1. Jacob Rupertus single-barreled pocket pistol.
2. Rollin White pocket pistol with a unique swivel breech.
3. A J. T. Stafford single-shot .22 caliber pistol with original holster.
4. Dexter Smith patent single-shot, .22 caliber breechloading pistol.
5. Rupertus single-shot .38 caliber breechloading pistol
6. F. Schoop patent two-shot "harmonica" .30 caliber rimfire pocket pistol.

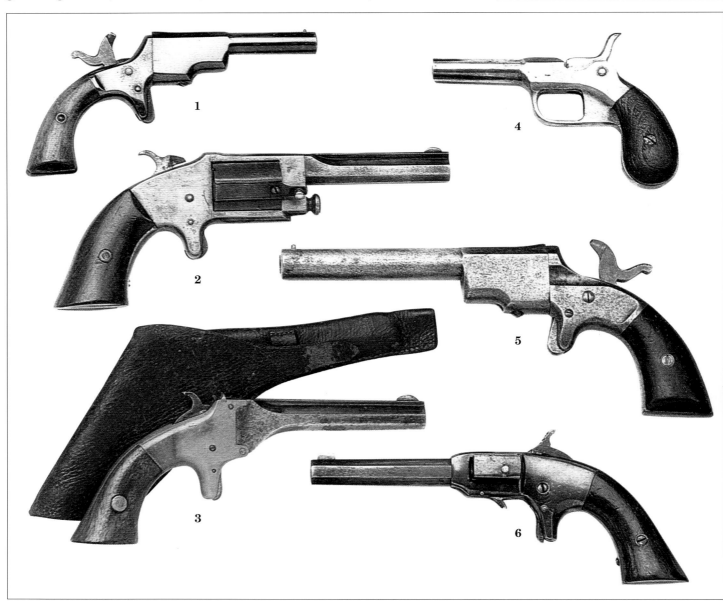

KEY:

1. A Sharps & Co. .32 caliber four-barrel pocket pistol. By depressing the button at the front of the frame, with the pistol at half-cock, the barrel could be pushed forward to load or eject the cartridges.
2. A later version of the Sharps four-barrel model with a bird's head grip.
3. William Marston's three-shot pocket pistol.
4. Later version of the Marston pistol.
5. Dickinson .32 caliber single-shot pistol. The ratchet is the extractor.
6. Late Sharps four-barrel pocket pistol with bird's head grip.
7. Frank Wesson's two-shot pistol. Center "barrel" sometimes contained a small "dirk."
8. .22 caliber long cased rimfire ammunition.
9. Two .32 caliber rounds.
10. Remington-Elliot .32 caliber rimfire four-barrel ring trigger "deringer", sometimes called "pepperbox."
11. Remington double "deringer" (s.n. 99745) shown opened.
12. A Sharps four-barrel pistol with checkered walnut stock.
13. Similar pistol but with Gutta-Percha grips.
14. Version of the Marston three-barrel pistol.
15. Eben T. Starr's four-barrel "pepperboxes" were rivals to the Sharps version.
16. Remington's "Saw Handle" "deringer" (c.1865) was produced in rimfire calibers from .30 to .41.
17. David Williamson's .41 rimfire "deringer" was modeled upon Henry Deringer's original. Unique in having a percussion insert when fixed ammunition was not available.

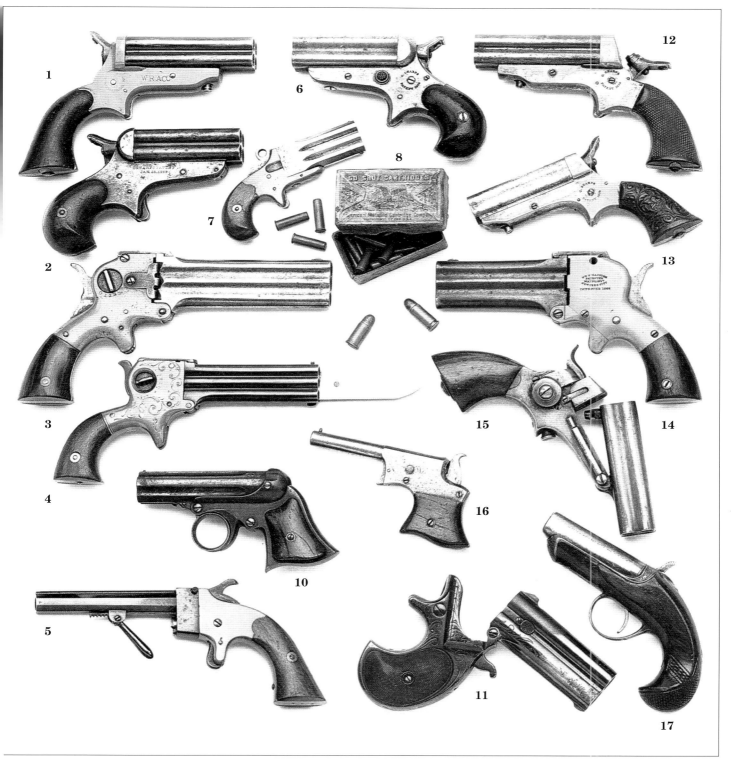

(Artifacts courtesy of Buffalo Bill Historical Center, Cody, Wyoming.)

COLT "DERINGERS" AND POCKET PISTOLS

The Colt Patent Firearms Manufacturing Company was not slow to go into the Deringer and small pocket pistol field as soon as self-contained cartridges became available. Having suffered setbacks with the death of Sam Colt in 1862, and a devastating factory fire in 1864, the company entered the market that had been created by the expansion of the Western frontier and the growth of

crime in developing urban areas.

The Colt Deringers and pocket pistols maintained the company's traditional innovation and design and high quality of manufacture. Its First and Second model Deringer pistols, made from 1870 to 1890, used the potent .41in caliber rimfire cartridge, and featured a barrel which pivoted to the side for easy loading. This movement also auto-

matically ejected the used cartridge case. In addition, its shape and weight were such that the user's fist could be wrapped around it, with the gun serving as a "knuckle duster," as the backup to firing the gun's single cartridge.

Including the Third Model, which was made from 1870 to 1912, Colt produced a total of about 63,000 Deringers. The name was used

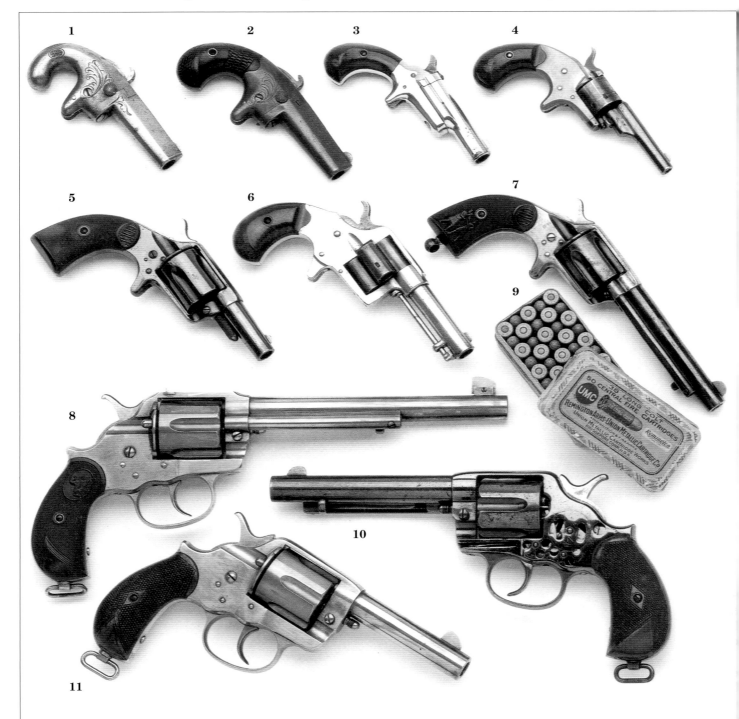

(Artifacts courtesy of Gene Autry Western Heritage Museum, Los Angeles, California.)

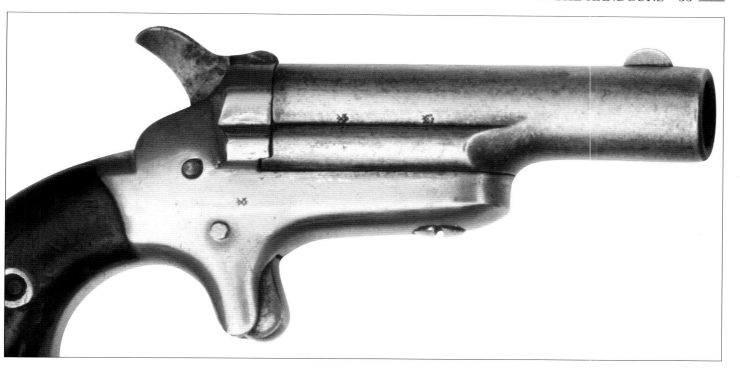

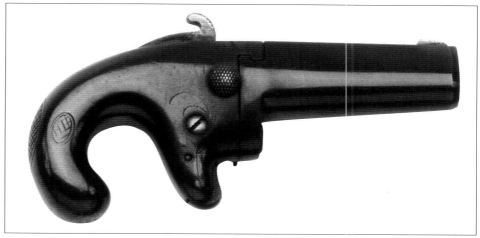

Top: *An example of Colt's Third Model Deringer: length overall, 4.8in; barrel, 2.5in. It was a .41in caliber weapon with a brass frame and bird's head grip.*

Above: *Colt's First Model Deringer. Firearms of this type were often carried as a second, concealed weapon as a back-up to a revolver visible in a holster.*

specifically to reflect Henry Deringer's original percussion pistol. However, other manufacturers often used the generic term "Derringer," such as Remington with its two-shot model (see illustration under The Handgun in the West and Frontier).

Colt also produced a series of its traditional revolvers as small, concealable pistols suitable for self-defense or backup purposes. As a rather odd transition from the single-shot Deringer to the full-scale revolver, the Cloverleaf House model had a four-shot cylinder in the shape of a cloverleaf, in the large .41in caliber like the Deringer. It was also the first Colt revolver with a solid frame across the top of the cylinder and also introduced the innovation of countersunk chambers to hold the rimmed cartridges. The weapon was introduced in 1874, and was followed in 1881 by the more conventional .38in caliber New House model. The name was obviously chosen to emphasize the use of the pistol for self-defense, at a time of large urban populations with corresponding crime rates.

The rest of the Colt small pistol models were grouped under the name of New Line. They ranged from .22in caliber, particularly suitable for women, to a five-shot model in .41in caliber.

Colt ultimately could not compete with the flood of cheaply made "Suicide Special" pistols prevalent in the 1890s. It is interesting to note that by that time the Old West of the frontier no longer existed, but the popularity of the full size Colt handguns originally developed for use on the Western frontier persisted, and remains to this day.

KEY:

1. *New Line Pocket Model revolver, .22 caliber, nickel with pearl grips, 1876, backstrap engraved "J.M. Foote, Jr."*
2. *New Line Pocket Model revolver, .32 caliber rimfire, 1880.*
3. *Model revolver, for the .38 caliber rimfire New Line, unfinished and stamped M.*
4. *New Line revolver, .41 caliber rimfire, 1874, five-shot cylinder.*
5. *Model 1877 Double Action Lightning revolver, .38 caliber, backstrap engraved "Capt. Jack Crawford," used by this well-known scout and "poet laureate" of the plains.*
6. *Model 1877 Double Action Lightning revolver, .41 caliber, blue finish with pearl grips.*
7. *Model 1877 Double Action Lightning revolver, caliber .38, engraved with ivory grips, with longer barrel and attached ejector rod.*
8. *Hammerless Model 1878 Double Action, an experimental version which did not go into production. Serial number 1.*
9. *Standard production 1878 Double Action Frontier revolver, .45 caliber, 7¹/₂ in barrel.*
10. *.44 S & W cartridges.*
11. *Experimental prototype Double Action revolver with swingout cylinder, no serial number, patented 1884. Five years later Colt issued first production swingout cylinder revolver, a mechanism similar to many used in the West from 1889 to the present day.*

Top left: *Colt's New Line Pocket Model in .22in caliber and with 2.2in octagonal barrel complete with foresight, with a long groove along the top of the solid frame to act as a backsight. Colt's Open Top and New Line .22 revolvers were made from 1873 to 1880, in .30, .32, .38 and .41in calibers, with barrels up to 4in long; total quantity, about 35,000.*

Above: *Third Model Deringer, one of thousands produced by Colt's from 1870 to 1912. They were single-shot weapons firing .41in caliber rimfire, with pivoting barrels for loading. About 63,000 First, Second, and Third Model Deringers were produced in all.*

Left: *Colt's New Line Pocket Model inscribed: "COLT NEW LINE" on left side of barrel, ".41 Cal" on the lower left frame, and with the company's name inscribed on the 2in barrel.*

Right: *A fine factory-engraved Colt Model 1849 Pocket pistol made in the early 1850s. Starting in 1849, this very popular sidearm had a die rolled cylinder scene showing a stagecoach driver routing six holdup men with his Colt revolver, which of course was a six-shot repeater.*

THE COLT SINGLE ACTION ARMY

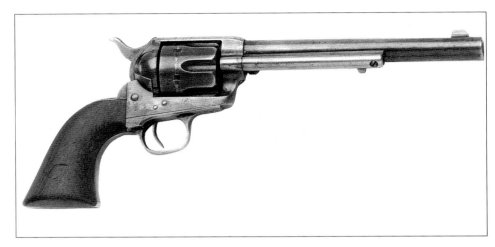

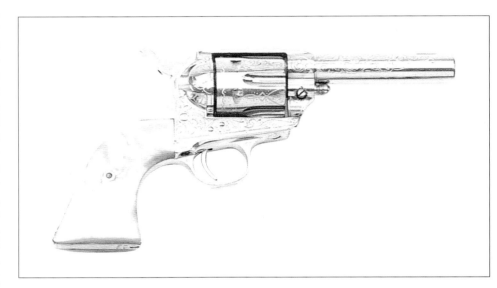

Few firearms were as easily identified with the gunfighter and the settlement of the West as the Colt Single Action Army revolver. Even its nicknames convey impressions of frontier lawmen and gunmen. Known variously as the "Peacemaker," the "Frontier Six-Shooter," the "Thumb Buster," and the "Hog Leg," this gun was popularly used and relied upon by men and women on both sides of the law and by both civilians and the military after its first release in 1872. Later, its legend lived on in countless Western movies.

Ironically, the Colt Single Action Army was brought out long after Smith & Wesson pioneered the development of revolvers using self-contained cartridges instead of the old percussion system. The reason for the delay on Colt's part was what historian R. L. Wilson has described as the major blunder of Sam Colt's professional life. In 1855 an employee of his, Rollin White, came up with the idea of having the revolver cylinder bored through from end to end, which would allow a self-contained cartridge. Sam Colt rejected the idea. White obtained a patent in 1855 and turned it over to Smith & Wesson. Later, after Smith & Wesson produced its .32in caliber Old Model Army revolver, which was used in the Civil War, the Colt company was offered a license, but at an exorbitant price which Colt rejected.

Starting in 1868, Colt's made strenuous efforts to convert its .44in Model 1861 Army revolver to cartridge use without infringing on the Rollin White patent. The Thuer conversion had the cartridges loaded from the front. The Richards conversion, manufactured as the White patent was expiring, loaded the cartridges from the rear but interposed a shield between the cartridges and the firing pin. These had some success, but surviving examples are now rare.

When the Colt Model 1873 Single Action Army was finally introduced (as the Model P, quickly given by Colt's dealers the popular term "Peacemaker"), the U.S. Army, facing widespread unrest among Native Americans tribes, was keenly interested. The Colt product won a com-

petition with the Smith & Wesson First Model American revolver and others. Ordnance Department notes of June 26, 1873, include the following entry: "As the reports . . . plainly show the superiority of the Colt revolver (last model) over all other tried, the Chief of Ordnance has been authorized by War Department to purchase 8,000 of these arms for the cavalry arm of the service."

The Single Action Army in .45in caliber with a 7.5in barrel was issued to the Army as the standard cavalry sidearm and was used at Custer's last stand at the Little Bighorn. The Army switched to a double action Colt revolver in .38in caliber in 1892 but, recognizing its inadequate stopping power, recalled many of the cavalry's Single Action Armys for refurbishment and reuse. With a cut-down barrel length of 5.5in, these were called the "Artillery Model" and were used in the Spanish-American War and in the

Top: *A Single Action Army with a 7.5in barrel in .41in caliber. In the Single Action Army the hammer had to be pulled rearwards to the cocked position, using the thumb or free hand, each time the weapon was to be fired.*

Above: *A "Sheriff's Model" with pearl grips and heavy scroll engraving by Cuno A. Helfritch, who was active with Colt from 1863 to 1921.*

Philippine Insurrection.

Under the name "Peacemaker," the Single Action Army was sold on the civilian market in many calibers and barrel lengths, and has continued to be produced by Colt's ever since 1873, except for a hiatus between 1940 and 1956. In popular literature it shares the title of "The Gun That Won The West" with the Winchester Model 1873 lever-action rifle.

The Single Action Army's design was adapted starting in 1877 for double action operation, with the

Lightning, the Thunderer (a .41in caliber version), and the Frontier. While criticized for not being as rugged as the Peacemaker, the Frontier in particular was popular, and its production approached the number of Peacemakers up to 1905. The Bisley, named after the English target shooting center, was a version of the Peacemaker introduced in 1894 with special target sights.

All Colt Single Action revolvers that were made before the introduction of smokeless powder in 1898 are highly sought after in today's active collectors' market. They were made in calibers from .32in to .45in and with barrel lengths up to 7.5in. The larger calibers and longer barrel lengths are especially in demand, as well as those fitted with wood grips as against the later hard rubber.

A variation of the Single Action Army is the Storekeeper's or

Below: *Standard production 1878 Double Action Lightning in .45in caliber and fitted with a 7.5in barrel.*

Bottom: *One of the finest Model 1878 Frontier Double Action Revolvers, in .45in caliber and with a 5.5in barrel. Decoration, by Cuno A. Helfritch in 1883, included elaborate scrolls, ribbons, wriggle lines, dots, florals, banners, and cross-hatching, with a rare panel scene depicting a tropical village.*

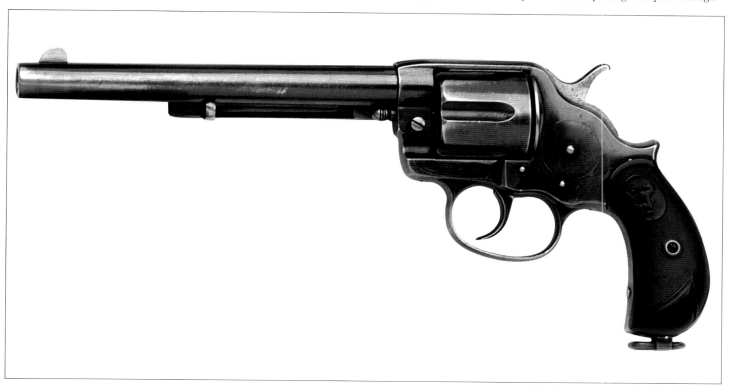

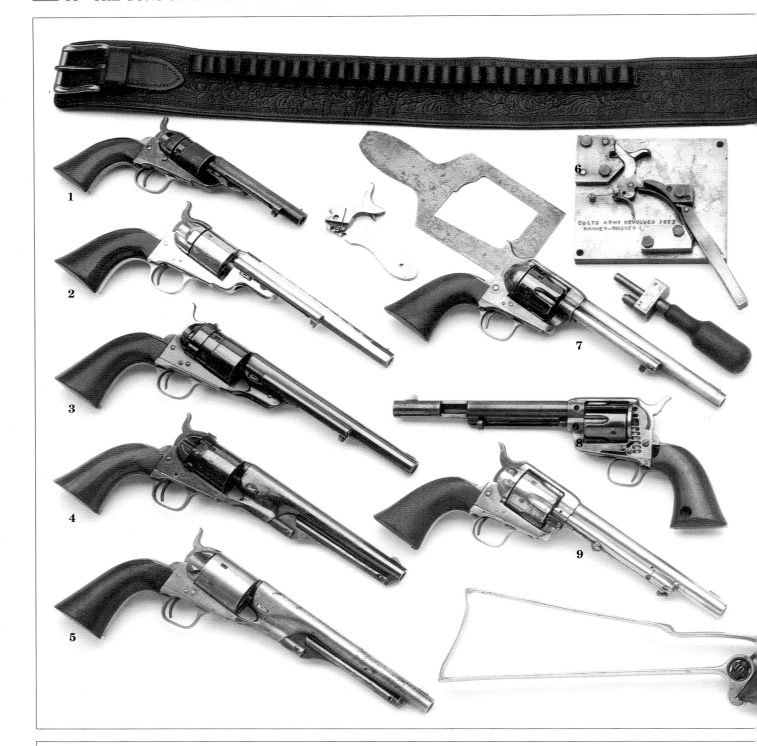

KEY:

1. Model 1862 Pocket Navy revolver, .36 caliber centerfire, c. 1873.
2. Model 1851 Navy conversion from .36 caliber percussion to .38 caliber rimfire, about 1873.
3. Richards-Mason Colt conversion revolver.
4. Thuer conversion of Model 1861 Navy revolver from percussion to front loading, tapered brass cased cartridge, .36 caliber, c. 1869.
5. Experimental .44 rimfire Colt cartridge revolver, c. 1868-9,
6. Gauges used for initial manufacture of the Colt Single Action Army revolver, 1872-4.
7. Serial number 1, "s" Colt Single Action

Army, the first manufactured in 1872, shipped to England for promotional purposes.
8. Factory cutaway Single Action, .45, showing internal mechanism
9. Experimental .45 caliber Single Action with automatic cartridge extractor.
10. Typical, inexpensive. machine-embossed holster and belt for Single Action Army Colt.
11. Gold-plated, pearl steer head grips, and with silver inlaid name on the backstrap, "Albert W. Bonds."
12. Box for .45 Colt cartridges, made by Remington-U.M.C.
13. Brass-cased .44 Smith & Wesson cartridges.
14. Nickel plated, ivory gripped Colt Single

Action .45 known to collectors as the "Sheriff's" model, was manufactured without the cartridge elector.
15. Carved Mexican eagles on ivory grips were especially popular south of the border where the Colt Single Action Army .45 became a weapon of choice.
16. Although available in many barrel lengths, the 4 3/4 in. model such as this .45 nickel-finished version was among the most popular of the Single Action Colts.
17. Colt Single Actions with detachable shoulder stocks and extra-long barrels could be ordered from the factory. This example was the first made, 1876.
18. Wells Fargo Express ordered a number of these .45 Colts for use by security

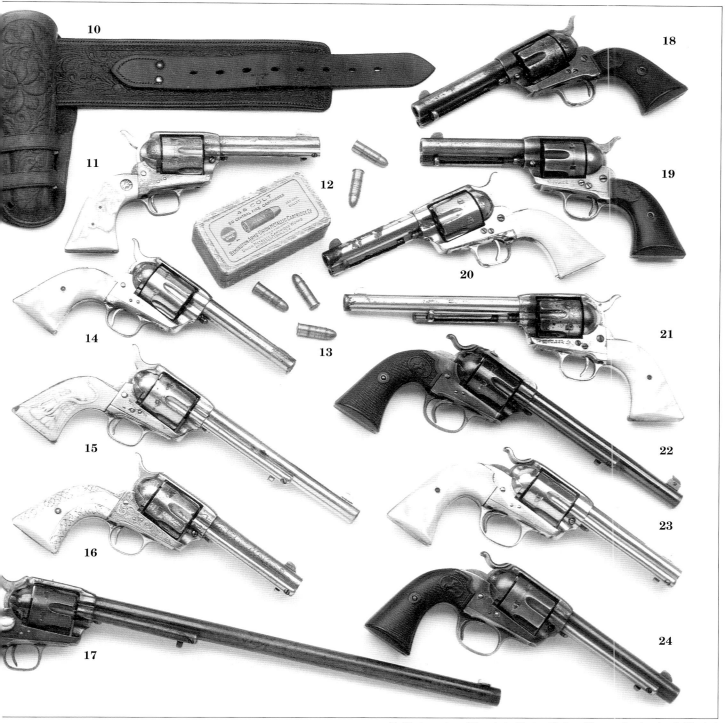

personnel in 1909.

19. *The same weapon proved reliable for Adams Express Company.*

20. *A .45 caliber Colt, with factory ivory grips decorated with carving.*

21. *Second in popularity to the .45, the .44-40 received wide use.*

22. *With longer curved grips and special target sights, the Bisley Model Single Action gained popularity in England and the United States.*

23. *With fixed sights and custom finish and grips, the Bisley also saw use in the West.*

24. *Standard Bisley model with fixed sights and 5 1/2 in. barrel.*

Sheriff's Model, with the barrel shortened to about 4in and with no ejector rod under the barrel. Another variation, with about 925 made, was the Flattop Target Model, with calibers down to .22in and cartridges up to 450 Boxer and 450 Eley. A variant of this was the notorious "Buntline Special," with an oversized 12 to 16in barrel. The term was actually invented by writer of Westerns in the 1930s, Edward Judson, who had "Ned Buntline" giving these to actual Dodge City lawmen. However, there is a record, according to R. L. Wilson, of an order for one by

Buckskin Frank Leslie in 1881, an actual Tombstone, Arizona gambler and bartender.

The massive Frontier Model pictured here was the last Colt revolver made before the more modern swingout cylinder models introduced in 1889. With this type, which continues today, the cylinder unlatches and pivots to the side, allowing simultaneous ejection and faster loading. The Army ordered 4,600 of a version of the Frontier with an oversized triggerguard, allowing use with gloves, popularly known as the Alaska Model.

COLT'S CARTRIDGE COMPETITORS

Smith & Wesson was Colt's major competitor in the Old West period after the introduction of large caliber cartridge revolvers. In 1870, having had a head start through its control of the Rollin White patent, Smith & Wesson introduced its First Model Single Action in .44in caliber, and sold 1,000 of these to the Army. A number of famous Western figures including Buffalo Bill Cody and Wyatt Earp carried this model. It featured a top break barrel that would pivot forward, automatically ejecting used cartridges. This was followed by a .45in caliber variation called the Schofield, after an Army Major who invented an improved catch for the pivoting barrel,

attached to the frame rather than to the top strap. The Army bought about 5,000 of these, and noted outlaws as such as the James brothers and Cole Younger, as well as U.S. Marshal Bill Tilghman, were reported as carrying this model. As mentioned above, however, Smith & Wesson lost out to the Colt Single Action Army in the military trials in 1873 for the major cavalry sidearm. The faster unloading was noted, but the Colt was considered to be better constructed, with fewer and more durable parts.

Remington produced a Single Action Army model in 1875 in .4in and .45in caliber. This attained some popularity, but was not purchased in

any quantity by the Army, Colt having secured the major contracts. It is readily identified by the triangular web under the loading lever, which is the same configuration as the Remington Army percussion revolvers that were the major competitor to Colt's firearms in the Civil War. The distinctive Remington cartridge pistol can be seen in numerous Western movies, evidently to provide some variety.

Another competitor in the large caliber "Army" field was the Merwin & Hulbert, made in .44in caliber between 1876 and 1880. The manufacturer was Hopkins & Allen of Norwich, Connecticut. It had a unique extraction and loading mech-

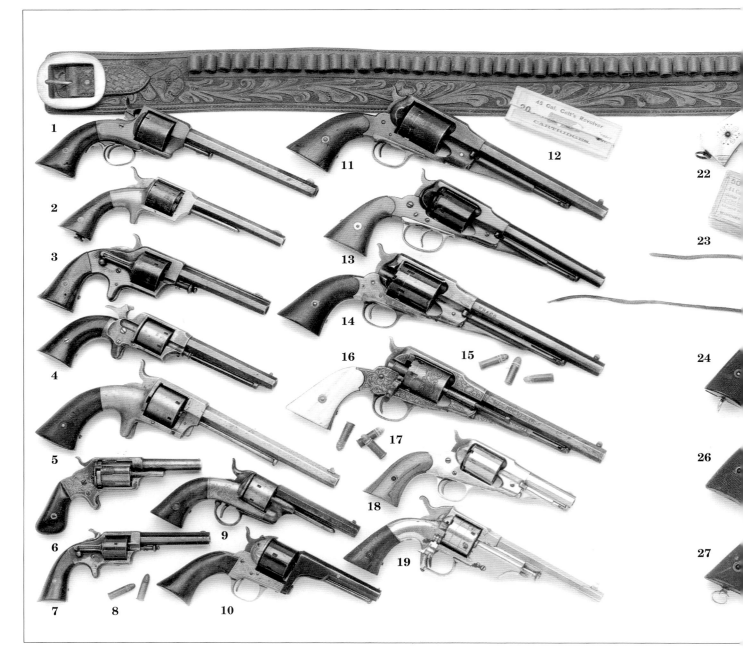

(Artifacts courtesy of Buffalo Bill Historical Center, Cody, Wyoming.)

anism in which the barrel with a top strap twisted sideways and when pulled forward activated a star-shaped extractor for used cartridges. Merwin & Hulbert were dealers and promoters, but did not succeed in obtaining any government contracts.

Above: *Remington's excellent first cartridge revolver, which appeared in 1875, differed very little in general appearance from the firm's earlier percussion arm. Major mechanical differences were the bored-through cylinder, the loading gate, and the provision of a Colt-type ejector rod working in a sleeve.*

KEY:
1. Prescott single action six-shot Navy revolver in .38 caliber rimfire.
2. Pond pocket or belt pistol.
3. Merwin & Bray pocket pistol.
4. Uhlinger pocket revolver (sometimes credited to W. L. Grant) in .32 rimfire.
5. Bacon's Navy revolver, six-shot .38 rimfire.
6. Brooklyn Firearms Co.'s "Slocum" pocket pistol in .32 rimfire.
7. Eagle Arms Company cup primed pocket revolver.
8. Two .22 caliber cartridges.
9. Bacon's .32 caliber rimfire pocket pistol. Short-lived because of infringement of Smith & Wesson's rights to bored-through cylinders.
10. Moore's "Seven-Shooter" .32 caliber rimfire pocket revolver.
11. Remington New Model Army 1863 converted from percussion to cartridge.
12. Box of .45 caliber ammunition from Colt's Army revolver.
13. Remington double action New Model belt pistol.
14. Remington New Model Army pistol converted to metallic cartridge.
15. Three .44 Remington cartridges.
16. A factory conversion of the 1863 Army revolver, engraved and fitted with ivory stocks.
17. Further Remington rounds.
18. Remington's No. 2 pocket revolver.
19. Allen & Wheelock's center hammer lipfire revolver. Notches were cut into the rear of the chambers to allow the hammer face to strike the cartridge "lips."
20. Belts complete with cartridge loops became common by the late 1870s. This ornate version is quite late.
21. The holster may not be contemporary to the belt, but it is of the type in common usage then.
22. Merwin & Hulbert's open top Army revolver. This well-made pistol, beaten by the Colt Peacemaker in trials, was popular out West.
23. Box of reloadable cartridges made at the government's Frankford Arsenal.
24. Merwin & Hulbert's Army pistol, nickel-plated.
25. Government-made cartridges.
26. Merwin & Hulbert's Army pistol with top strap.
27. Remington Model 1890 single action Army revolver. About 2,000 were made.
28. Box of Winchester-made cartridges for Colt's .45 Double and Single Action Army revolvers.
29. Smith & Wesson's No. 3 Model Army pistol in .44 caliber "Russian," so called because of special ammunition ordered by the Russians.
30. Smith & Wesson No. 3 "American" Model.
31. Schofield version of the Model No. 3 with improved barrel latch.
32. Smith & Wesson New Model No. 3 revolver in .44 Russian caliber.
33. .44 Russian cartridge.
34. Smith & Wesson's .44 double-action 1881 "Frontier" revolver.

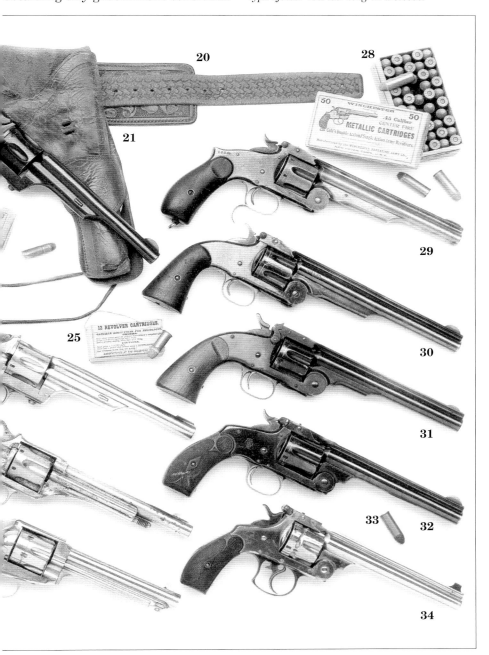

HANDGUNS AND HOLSTERS

Those in the West who armed themselves with a handgun needed some kind of container or holster to make carrying the weapon comfortable and to ensure that the firearm would be protected and easy to draw when needed. Single-shot percussion or flintlock pistols prior to the 1830s could be carried in a belt sash or might have a metal clip on the side to hook the gun onto the belt. In the 1830s it was common for both military and civilian personnel to drape a pair of pommel holsters over the front of the saddle to carry pistols and holsters on horseback. Civilian use of pommel or saddle bags which had built-in holsters con-

tinued until well after the turn of the twentieth century.

As the number of handguns proliferated, holster styles rapidly developed and changed. Earlier civilian styles reflected military influences in the use of flap covers. Saddle makers manufactured holster styles which in the 1860s and 1870s were form fitting and held the revolver snugly and safely in place.

Most flap holsters used by the cavalry were made to be worn on the right hip, with the butt facing forward. Thus the trooper could draw the pistol with his left hand, keeping the right hand free for his saber. Alternatively, if he wanted to keep

one hand on the reins and use only his revolver, he could draw underhand with his right hand, keeping the left for the reins (also a safer maneuver, with the pistol staying clear of the horse's neck).

There was a major change in holster design in the 1870s, when the earlier percussion revolvers were replaced by cartridge guns. These avoided exposed caps and loading levers, and were more reliable for fast shooting. A separate skirt was used with the user's belt looped through slits at the top, the holster itself being held with straps below. This is the type commonly seen in Western movies. A later change,

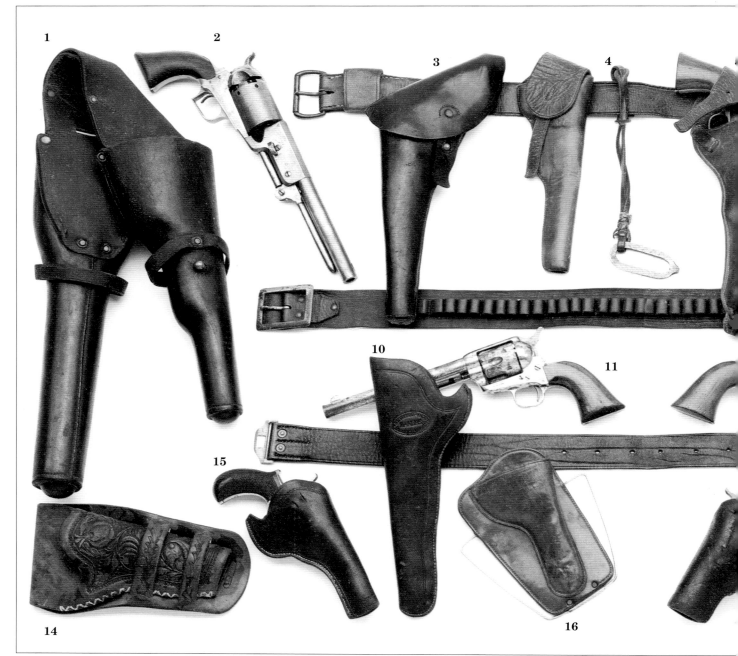

(Artifacts courtesy of Gene Autry Western Heritage Museum, Los Angeles, California.)

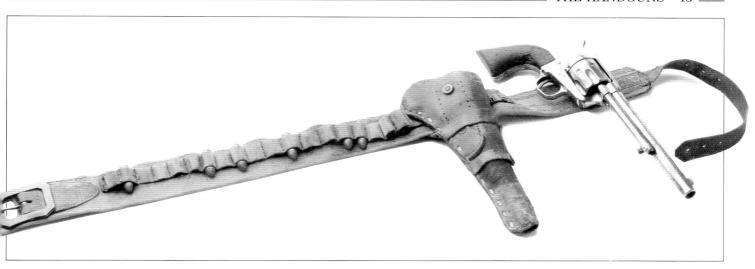

which did not take place until the turn of the century, was to widen the skirt at the top, in what was called called the "buscadero" style.

Above: *A Colt Single Action Army revolver, the famed Peacemaker/Frontier, with double-loop holster and belt containing .45in caliber centerfire cartridges.*

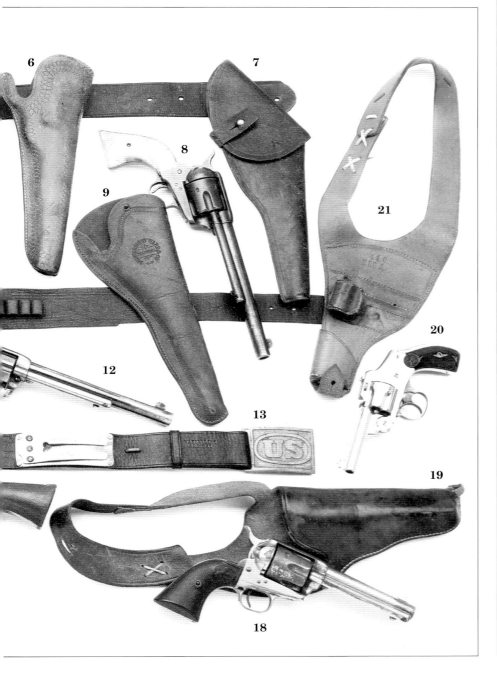

KEY:

1. *U.S. military issue pommel holsters for 1855 pistol carbine on one side and Colt Walker on the other, about 1855.*
2. *The Colt Walker's massive weight made it impractical to carry on the person. Pommel holsters were desirable for such revolvers.*
3. *Standard military issue flap holster used with Colt Dragoon and Army revolvers, 1850s-60s.*
4. *Civilian half-flap holster with an 1851 Colt Navy revolver, complete with belt and attached steel for starting fires.*
5. *Civilian half-flap holster for an 1861 Colt Army.*
6. *Form-fitting civilian holster, open top for 1860 Army.*
7. *Inexpensive civilian holster of the 1860s.*
8. *Mail-order Montgomery Ward holster for Colt Single Action Army revolver.*
9. *Typical Colt .45, also available by mail from Montgomery Ward.*
10. *Left-handed holster, about 1880, made in Dodge City, Kansas, by S. C. Gallup.*
11. *Colt .44-40 Frontier revolver.*
12. *Colt .45 Single Action, 1880s.*
13. *Experimental Bridgeport device, tested by the Army. An enlarged hammer screw on the revolver slid into the metal plate, holding the gun so that it could be pivoted and fired.*
14. *Typical civilian tooled holster for the Colt Single Action.*
15. *Belt holster for the Colt Lightning Double Action revolver.*
16. *Patented pocket holster for concealing double action revolver.*
17. *This 1860 .44 caliber Colt Army revolver and its matching holster have been cut down to create a powerful but concealable belt gun.*
18. *Colt Single Action Army .45 of the 1890s.*
19. *Shoulder holster for the Colt Single Action Army, 1890s.*
20. *Smith & Wesson hammerless double action revolver.*
21. *Shoulder holster.*

SHARPS RIFLES

As mentioned earlier, the muzzle-loading "Plains Rifle" was the prevailing type of longarm on the Western frontier up to the middle 1850s. In 1848, however, the young inventor Christian Sharps patented a practical breechloading rifle which attained instant popularity. Sharps had worked at the Harpers Ferry Armory under pioneering gunmaker John Hall, who had invented a workable but clumsy breechloading rifle as early as 1819, with a rising block actuated by a spring catch. Sharps' system used a falling block actuated by the trigger guard as a lever, fully uncovering the breech end of the barrel so that the powder and bullet could be inserted directly from the rear. Through the Civil War, the powder and bullet were placed in a linen or paper cartridge and ignition was by the hammer coming down on a separate percussion cap (or tape or pellet primer). After the war, the system was readily converted to use as a self-contained metal cartridge with the hammer actuating a firing pin.

The earliest Sharps rifles and carbines were produced for the inventor's company first by A. S. Nippes in Philadelphia and then by Robbins and Lawrence in Windsor, Vermont, which formed its own subsidiary in 1855 in Connecticut under the name of the Sharps Rifle Manufacturing

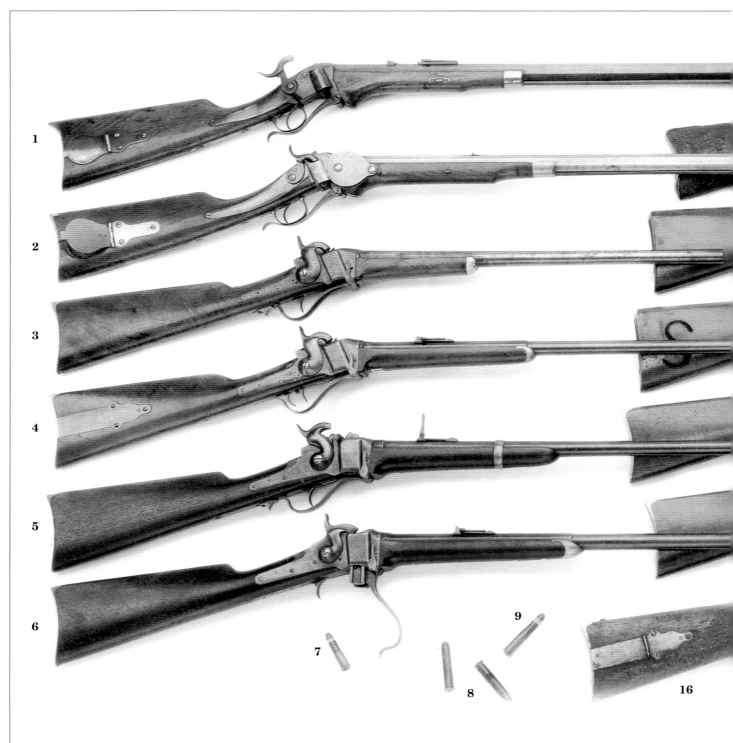

(Artifacts courtesy of Buffalo Bill Historical Center, Cody, Wyoming.)

Company. Christian Sharps himself went to Philadelphia, where he operated under the name of C. Sharps and Company, making pistols and Sharps & Hankins sliding breech carbines, until his death in 1874.

As the Civil War loomed in 1854, Sharps carbines were shipped into the Kansas territory by the Reverend Henry Ward Beecher and other abolitionists in crates marked "Bibles," with the guns becoming known as "Beecher's Bibles." John Brown also used Sharps carbines for

KEY:

1. *Sharps Model 1850 rifle, complete with Maynard's tape primer.*
2. *Model 1849 with circular disk automatic capping device.*
3. *Sharps Model 1852 carbine in .52 caliber and with slanting breech.*
4. *The rifle version complete with set triggers for targets and hunting.*
5. *Sharps 1869 carbine, produced in calibers as large as .60.*
6. *Rifle version of the Model 1869.*
7. *A .40-50 caliber Sharps cartridge. Both the percussion and the rimfire or centerfire versions could be loaded at speed.*
8. *.49-90 cartridge.*
9. *.44-70 cartridge.*
10. *This 1874 Sharps rifle has a repaired stock. Many rifles were prone to breakage at this point due to recoil.*
11. *Version of 1874 Model with blade foresight.*
12. *Fine Sharps in "as new" condition.*
13. *This rifle has normal rear sights on the barrel and peep or adjustable sights on the stock.*
14. *Round-barreled Sharps rifles were uncommon.*
15. *Box of .40 caliber shells 17/8in long,*
16. *New Model 1863 rifle.*
17. *Plains cartridge belt.*

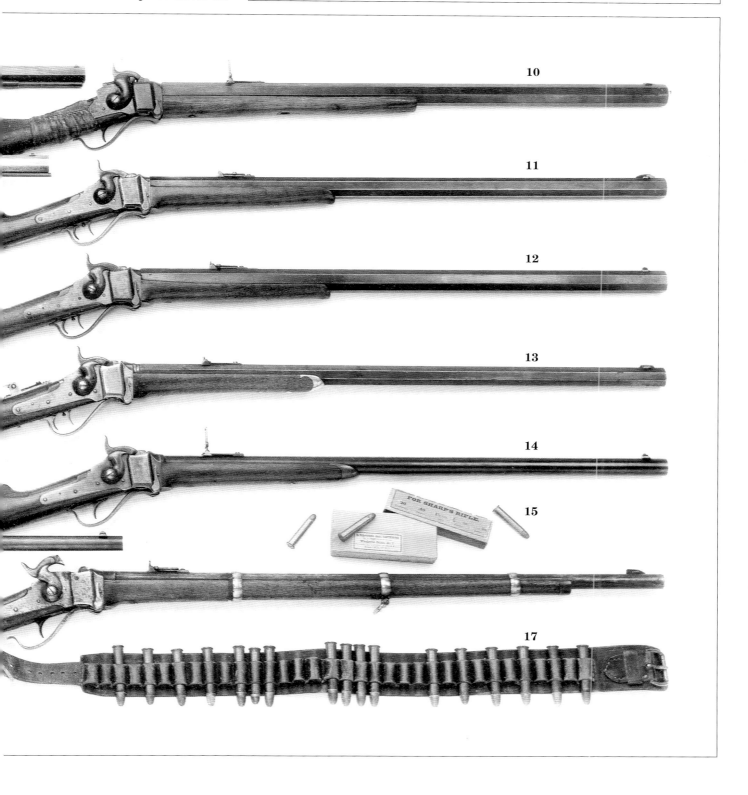

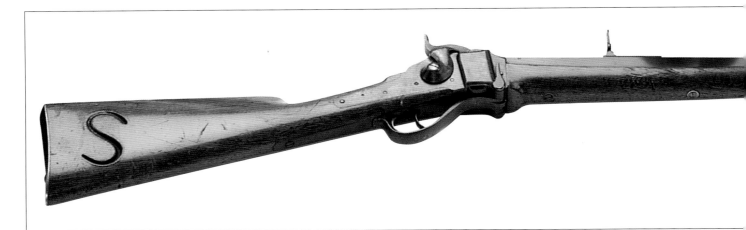

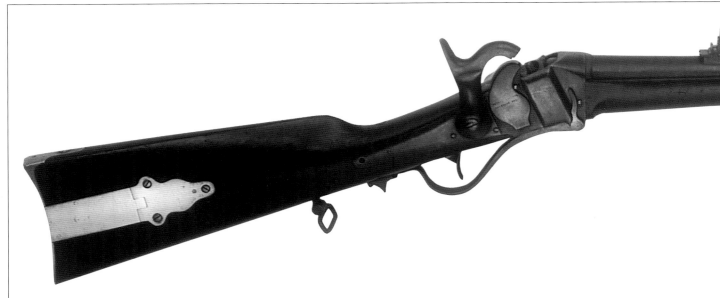

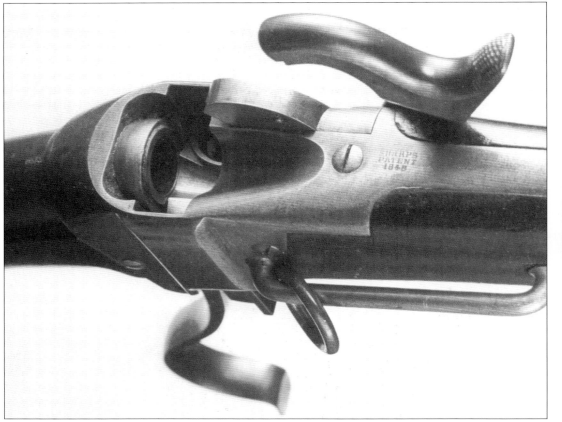

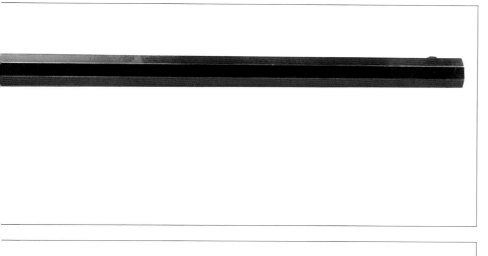

Left: Sharps Model 1874 carbine, a 0.45in caliber weapon with heavy octagonal barrel. The branded "S" on the butt is an owner's rather than a maker's mark.

Below, left: Sharps carbine, in which a made-up cartridge of powder and bullet were wrapped in some combustible material, loaded into the breech, and then fired by a separate percussion cap.

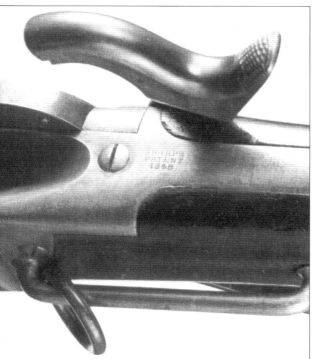

Far left: Sharps "capping breechloader" mechanism, showing lever down and breech open to show the vertical movement of the block. Its upper edge sheared off the end of the cartridge to expose the powder to the flash. Many Sharps were later converted to centerfire and were popular with buffalo hunters.

Left: Breech closed, with the hammer at half-cock to show the nipple. The Sharps leaked some gas, but had the advantage of a dual means of ignition: it took the ordinary percussion cap and was also fitted with a tape primer, which took rolls of caps like those in today's children's toy pistols. A fresh one was pushed over the nipple when the hammer was cocked; thus a mounted man did not have to fumble with relatively small caps to prime.

his insurrection which ended at Harpers Ferry.

The British government purchased several thousand of the carbines for cavalry use, and when the Civil War began, well over 100,000 were purchased by the U.S. Ordnance Department. Somewhat fewer rifles were produced for use most famously by Berdan's Sharpshooters, most with double set triggers for extra accuracy. After the Civil War, many of the carbines were converted to metallic cartridge use.

Starting in 1874, the company (the original Sharps Rifle Manufacturing Company in Connecticut) produced a series of hunting rifles that became synonymous in the West with the "Buffalo Gun." With large calibers, including the .50 "Big Fifty," these rifles were well suited for long range operation. The near extinction of the buffalo, whose northern and southern herds numbered in the hundreds of thousands and supported the migratory Plains Indian tribes, is one of the saddest chapters in the history of the West. Among the famous buffalo hunters was William F. Cody, who provided buffalo meat for the workers on the new transcontinental railroad and was later known as "Buffalo Bill."

Many Sharps rifles and carbines found their way into the hands of Native Americans, and were used extensively in the Indian Wars. However, a famous example of the "Buffalo Gun" being used against the Native Americans was the Battle of the Adobe Walls in 1874, in which a group of Texas buffalo hunters stood off a much larger attacking force led by Quanah Parker. Young hunter Billy Dixon killed one of the raiding party with his Sharps at a distance estimated at over 1,500 yards.

SHARPS' COMPETITORS

Single-shot hunting rifles were popular in the West even after the advent of the Winchester lever-action repeater, one reason being that, at least until the Winchester Model 1886, they could take larger, longer range cartridges that were more effective for hunting. The western plains and mountains were teeming with big game ripe for hunting, including deer, antelope, elk, and bear, in addition to the buffalo.

Sharps' leading competitor for buffalo hunting was the Remington "Rolling Block" sporting rifle, which was made from 1868 to 1888. With a two-piece stock, this rifle had an exceptionally strong action with a pivoting or "rolling' block ahead of the hammer, moved by a projecting ear. It was especially popular around the world as a military rifle, with over a million sold to various foreign countries. The finest model produced was the Long Range Creedmoor, named after the famous rifle range of that name on Long Island, New York.

The Ballard rifle, first produced in 1862 with a breech adaptable to either percussion or cartridge use,

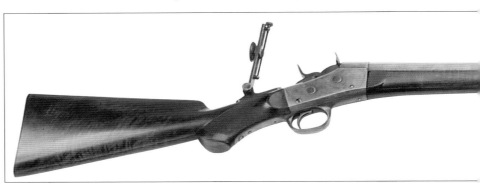

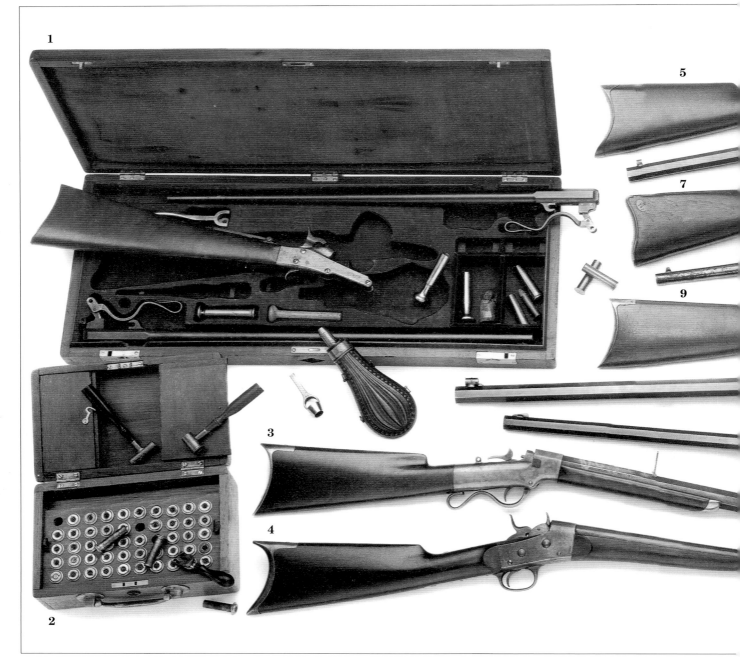

was later produced by the Marlin Firearms Company, and was known for its fine finish and accuracy. It was offered in nine models, with cartridges ranging from .38-50 to .45-100.

The Frank Wesson Company, which eventually became Harrington and

Richardson, produced still another variation, the "Two Trigger" model, from 1859 to 1888. The second trigger released a catch which allowed the barrel to tip downward so that the breech moved upward to expose it for loading. Another Wesson was made with a single trigger, an outside ham-

Below, left: *Remington-Creedmore rifle, once owned by George Armstrong Custer. With a 0.44-100 caliber, it was one of the finest weapons ever made by Remington. The basic "rolling block" mechanism was patented in 1863 by inventor Leonard Geiger, who was subsequently employed by the company. Some Remingtons were made for use in the Civil War, but were completed too late to see action. Improvements were made to the system thereafter, and in 1867 it was voted finest rifle in the world at the Imperial Exposition in Paris.*

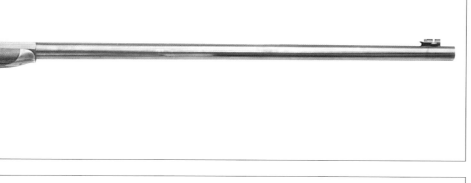

mer, and a falling block, with a more refined looking appearance than the Sharps. Designed for accuracy at long range, this rifle came with fine grade wood stocks and Vernier rear peep sights.

Winchester itself entered the single-shot rifle market, but only in 1885, with the rifle designed by John Browning. Variations of this famous rifle, which was produced up to 1920, were the High Wall and Low Wall. The Eli Whitney Company, a major gun manufacturer since 1798, introduced a single-shot rifle called the Phoenix in 1867, but Winchester ended competition from Whitney by buying the company in 1888.

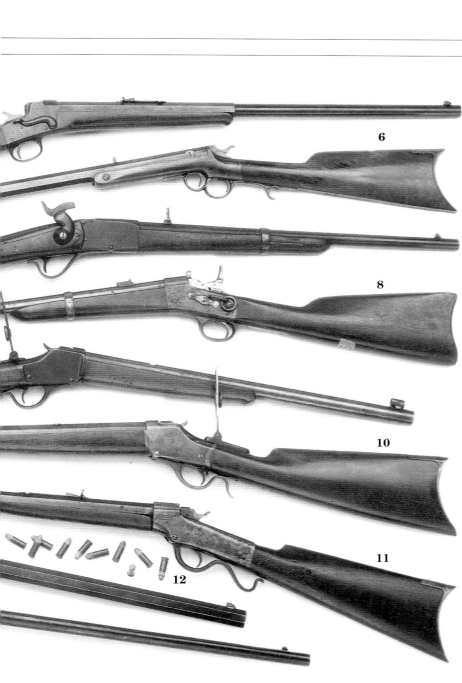

KEY:
1. *Maynard .50 caliber rifle in fitted case with reloading tools, powder flask, and cartridges. Note second barrel. These were normally supplied in different calibers from .32 to .44 rimfire or centerfire.*
2. *Cartridge box for the Maynard rifle.*
3. *Sturdy breechloader by the Brown Mfg Co.*
4. *Remington No. 1 Rolling Block sporting rifle. It was chambered for various calibers from .40 to .50; popular with hunters and plainsmen alike.*
5. *Remington-Hepburn rifle with pistol grip.*
6. *Fine example of Frank Wesson's two-trigger rifle.*
7. *The outside hammer Peabody hunting rifle appeared in calibers .44 to .46.*
8. *Remington Rolling Block short-range rifle in the "Light Baby Carbine" model.*
9. *Winchester single-shot rifle Model 1885 with a 20-inch round barrel.*
10. *Similar weapon fitted with 30-inch octagonal barrel. Both weapons have adjustable rear sights.*
11. *Fine Marlin-Ballard No. 2 sporting rifle in .38 centerfire.*
12. *.38 centerfire, shells for the Marlin-Ballard.*

COLT'S SHOULDER ARMS

When he opened his first factory in Paterson, New Jersey, Sam Colt thought, mistakenly, that revolving longarms had a greater future than handguns. The Army did buy 360 of the Model 1839 carbine, first produced in 1838, and these were used to good effect in the Seminole War of the same year. This brought Colt's arms to the attention of the Texans, who enabled Colt to start up again in Hartford after his Paterson business failed.

Before the Civil War, Colt sold the Army some 15,000 revolving rifles and carbines. The rifles were the original issue of the famed Berdan's Sharpshooters. Sporting models and shotguns were also introduced.

However, these percussion longarms could not be adapted for cartridge use, and also had the significant disadvantage that ignition would sometimes flash over between cylinders, leading to a simultaneous discharge that would put the shooter's forward hand at considerable risk.

With Winchester having pioneered the lever-action repeating rifle, and evidently due to Winchester's patents, the only longarm made by Colt's up to 1883 was a fine quality double-barreled shotgun, the Model 1878. This was a success until there was too much competition from less expensive foreign products. In 1883, Colt's introduced a new lever-action rifle, the Burgess, attempting to broaden the

market for Colt products. However, at a famous meeting between top executives of Colt and Winchester, the Winchester president, T. G. Bennett, exhibited a new revolver that had been designed by his employees, and suggested his company might produce it in competition with Colt. A "gentlemen's agreement" was promptly reached whereby Colt's would not produce lever-action rifles and Winchester would not produce revolvers. Production of the Burgess was immediately stopped, although Colt's did proceed with slide-action rifles called the Lightning, in Small, Medium, and Large frame models. In particular the Small Frame model in .22in caliber attained considerable

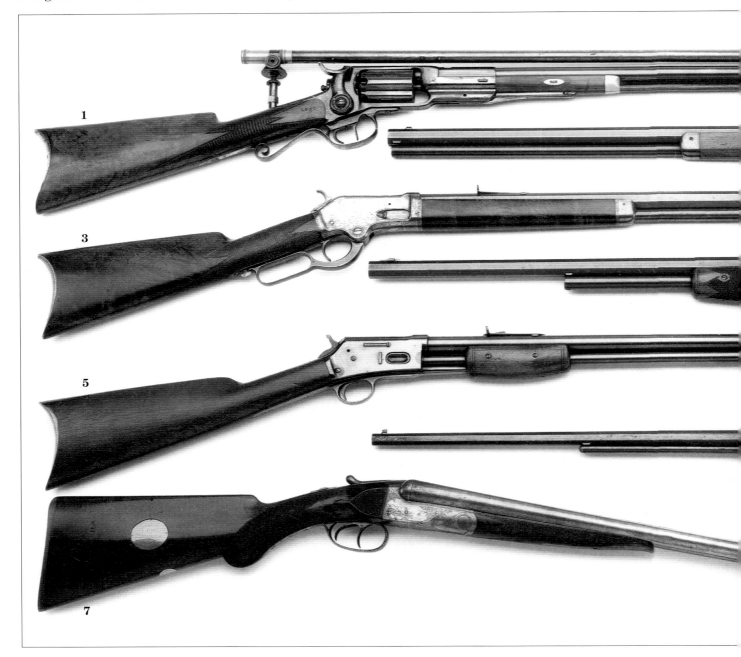

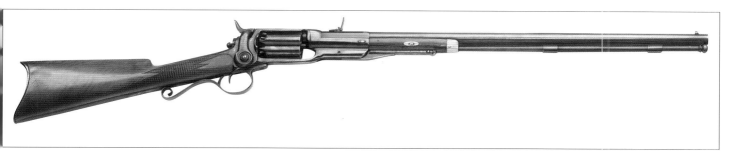

success up to 1898, and was so well made that some are still in use today. Ironically, although Colt's historically is known for handguns, today its major claim to fame is the ubiquitous AR-16 (M16) rifle.

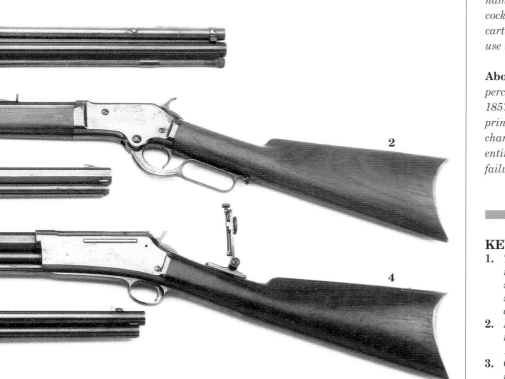

Top: *Fine example of the .58in caliber single-shot Model 1861 rifle-musket produced under contract by Colt's. It operated with a percussion cap and a paper cartridge, and a hammer on the side that had to be manually cocked. The firer would bite off the end of the cartridge, pour the powder in the muzzle, and use the ramrod to load the bullet.*

Above: *Colt Model 1855 rifle. This half-stock percussion sporting rifle was made between 1857 and 1864 and operated on the revolver principle, with four rounds in the revolving chamber. Such "revolver rifles" were never entirely successful, being prone to mechanical failure, not infrequently at the worst moment.*

KEY:
1. This half-stock Colt revolving sporting rifle of the Model 1855 is equipped with a sighting scope and has special finish and set triggers. It was the top of the Colt company's rifle line at the time.
2. Lever-action .44 caliber Colt Burgess rifle, manufactured between 1883 and 1885. Fewer than 7,000 were made.
3. Colt Burgess, deluxe engraved, inlaid with gold, presentation inscribed from the Colt factory to William F. "Buffalo Bill" Cody in 1883, the first year his famed Wild West show traveled to the East.
4. Lightning slide-action rifle, large frame, caliber .40-60-260, half magazine, peep sight.
5. Lightning slide-action rifle, medium frame, .44-40 caliber, purchased about 1898 for the San Francisco Police Department.
6. Lightning slide-action rifle, small frame, .22 caliber, 1890.
7. This hammerless Model 1883 Colt shotgun was a presentation from Samuel Colt's son Caldwell in about 1891.

VOLCANIC FIREARMS

The Volcanic lever action rifle (and pistol using the same system) was a spectacular invention but ahead of its time, since the self-contained cartridge had not been perfected. Its importance may be measured against the typical longarms of the time: all single-shot, and primarily muzzleloading.

The Volcanic has a convoluted history, involving two of the most famous names in gunmaking: Smith and Wesson. Walter Hunt, a New York inventor, had the first idea for a lever-action repeating rifle, which he patented in 1849. Called the "Volitional Repeater," it used a hol-low-based conical bullet which he called the "Rocket Ball," filled with powder and with the base closed by a cork wad having a hole in its center to admit the flame from an independent priming unit. There was a straight, spring-driven pin and a tubular magazine under the barrel, which had been features of lever-action rifles up to that time.

Not being able to finance further development, Hunt sold his rights to a group including Lewis Jennings, who carried the design further. An order was then placed with the Robbins and Lawrence factory in Windsor, Vermont, to have the rifles produced. Here Horace Smith and Daniel Wesson entered the picture. Working with Robbins and Lawrence in 1854, they patented an effective mechanism for moving the cartridge carrier and locking it in the forward position, which completed the essential mechanical features of the later Henry and Winchester rifles.

While the rifle did not sell well and production was curtailed, Smith and Wesson formed their own partnership in Connecticut and switched their attention to handguns using the same system, which they called the "Volcanic." After a year, however, the partnership was bought out by a

(Artifacts courtesy of Buffalo Bill Historical Center, Cody, Wyoming.)

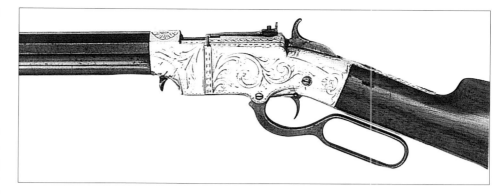

Right: *A fine Volcanic rifle, with brass frame finished in silver and gold plating. The name "Volcanic" reportedly originated as a nickname for the previous Smith & Wesson pistol-type arms; apparently it came from an article in* Scientific American *magazine in 1854, comparing the rapid fire capability of the gun with the fiery eruption of a volcano.*

group of investors including Oliver Winchester, a successful industrialist who owned a factory for making shirts. While a substantial arms factory was built, the company did not prosper, evidently due to the faulty "Rocket Ball" ammunition, which was low powered and tended to corrode the rifle barrels. The company went bankrupt in 1857 and Oliver Winchester became the sole owner.

The final chapter in the story was an astute move by Winchester in engaging Benjamin Tyler Henry to redesign both the rifle and the ammunition. This was the end of the Volcanic and the beginning of the Henry rifle and the Winchester empire.

However, before the dissolution of the first Smith and Wesson company, the foundation was laid for another arms making empire, still known as Smith & Wesson. In 1853 Horace Smith patented a self-contained cartridge based on Flobert's "saloon pistol" using a lead ball seated in a copper percussion cap. This became the .22in rimfire cartridge, and together with Daniel Wesson's invention of a revolver using this cartridge, patented in 1855, became the basis for the permanent Smith & Wesson Company.

The total production of the Volcanic rifles and pistols under both Smith and Wesson and Winchester is estimated at about 6,000, and these are now scarce collectors' items.

KEY:
1. *Pair of Hunt's patented .54 caliber "Rocket Balls."*
2. *Volcanic .38 caliber (.41 cartridge), 30-shot carbine (s.n. 88).*
3. *Trio of Volcanic No. 2 (.41 caliber) bullets.*
4. *Volcanic .30 caliber (.31 cartridge), 6-shot pistol (s.n. 1340).*
5. *Volcanic .38 caliber (.41 cartridge), 25-shot carbine (s.n. 82).*
6. *Volcanic .38 caliber (.41 cartridge), 10-shot pistol-carbine (s.n. 1342).*
7. *Smith & Wesson .30 caliber (.31 cartridge), 6-shot pistol (s.n. 44).*
8. *Volcanic .38 caliber (.41 cartridge), 20-shot carbine (s.n. 1).*
9. *Volcanic .30 caliber (.31 cartridge), 6-shot pistol (s.n. 1868).*
10. *Volcanic .38 caliber (.41 cartridge), 10-shot pistol (s.n. 1159).*
11. *Smith & Wesson .38 caliber (.41 cartridge), 10-shot pistol.*
12. *Box of 200 No. 2 (.41 caliber) Volcanic cartridges.*
13. *Volcanic .30 caliber (.31 cartridge), 10-shot target pistol (s.n. 1999).*
14. *Volcanic .38 caliber (.41 cartridge), 10-shot pistol (s.n. 1528).*
15. *Volcanic .38 caliber (.41 cartridge), 10-shot pistol (s.n. 1161).*
16. *Volcanic .38 caliber (.41 cartridge). 8-shot pistol (s.n. 822).*

THE HENRY RIFLE

The Henry rifle was derivative of the Smith & Wesson/Volcanic arms. Henry's modification of the action and improved cartridge revolutionized the concept. It consisted of a brass casing with the propellant in its base and a 216-grain bullet and 25 grains of powder. This "rimfire" proved successful and was modified several times. Ordnance tests were

Right: *A beautiful Henry rifle, serial number 6, presented to President Abraham Lincoln who by all accounts was both fascinated by firearms and a competent marksman.*

Below: *Seated, facing toward the reader's right, is F. D. Orcutt, a member of Co. A, 7th Illinois Color Guard, who owned Henry rifle number 4140.*

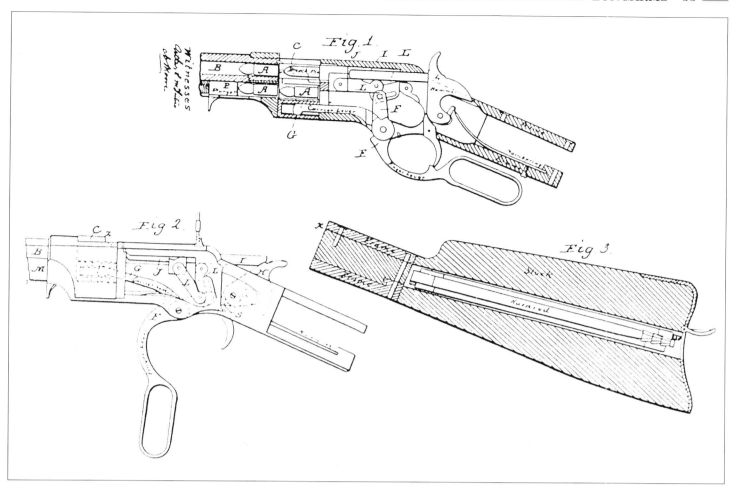

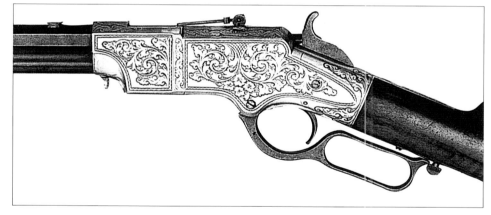

Above: *Details from the Henry patent drawings, October 16, 1860, showing the toggle link mechanism which was carried forward with Winchester rifles until the Model 1886 design by John Browning. The Henry set the pattern for all subsequent lever action rifles, albeit with changes to the cartridge loading system.*

Right: *Henry's are now highly collectible, particularly in heavily engraved form, such as this brass-framed example finished in silver and gold plating.*

encouraging and it was claimed that at 400 yards the bullet could embed itself 5 inches into a wooden target.

The U.S. government was tardy in accepting the Henry rifle, but by 1863 a large number of them had been issued to volunteer and state troops. Kansas in particular took to the Henry. It was reported in 1863 that Gen. James Blunt's bodyguards were to be armed with "Henry's Volcanic repeating rifles and two revolvers and will be mounted on picked horses." The Henry was fitted with a tubular magazine that could hold sixteen rounds. Its only drawback was its price: in October 1862 it was listed at $42, the ammunition at

$10 per thousand. Even the dealers failed to get a good discount but demand was sufficient to keep the company busy. A major weakness was its exposed magazine spring which necessitated loading it from the muzzle end. In 1866 this was rectified by placing a slot in the side of the receiver and spring pressure from the muzzle end. Too late for the Henry, it was incorporated instead in its successor, the Winchester Model 1866.

Another problem was that Brigadier General James W. Ripley, the elderly Chief of Ordnance, resisted all innovations and felt that a repeating rifle would make the troops

waste ammunition (the magazine actually held fifteen rounds, but another could be held in the chamber).

Where the rifle was used in Civil War combat, it was extremely effective: the only full regiment equipped with Henry rifles, Colonel Lafayette C. Baker's First Washington, D.C., Cavalry, routed a large force of Confederates on a raid on Petersburg and took sixty prisoners. At the Battle of Allatoona Pass, Georgia, a smaller group of Federal troops armed with Henrys held off a Confederate force outnumbering them three to two, and exacted a casualty rate second only to Gettysburg.

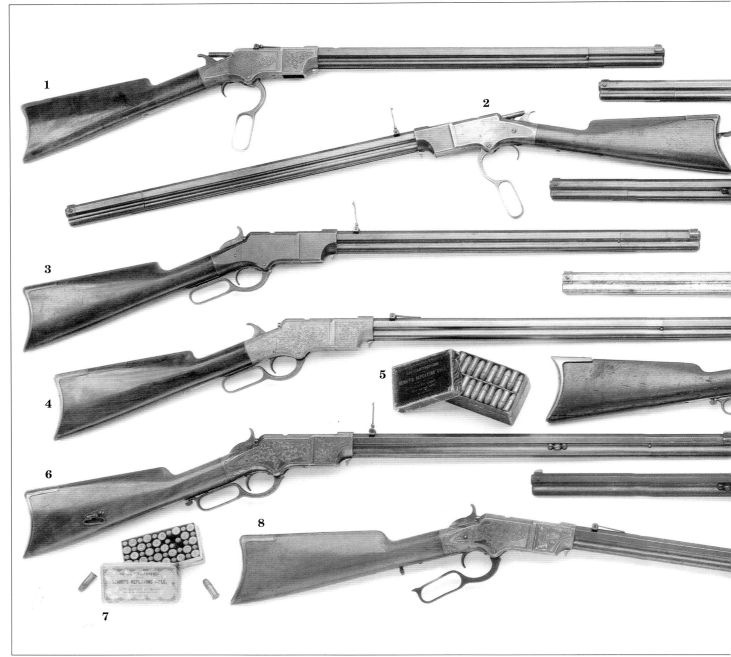

(Artifacts courtesy of Buffalo Bill Historical Center, Cody, Wyoming.)

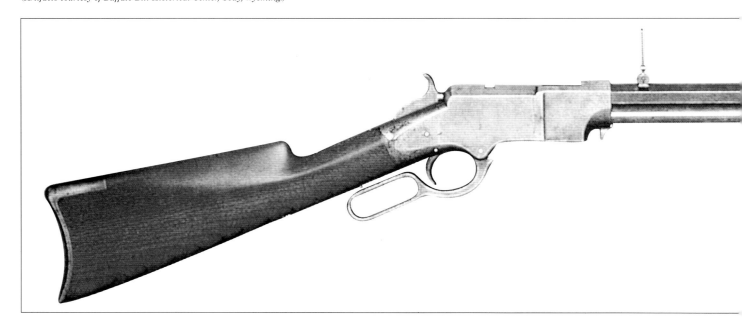

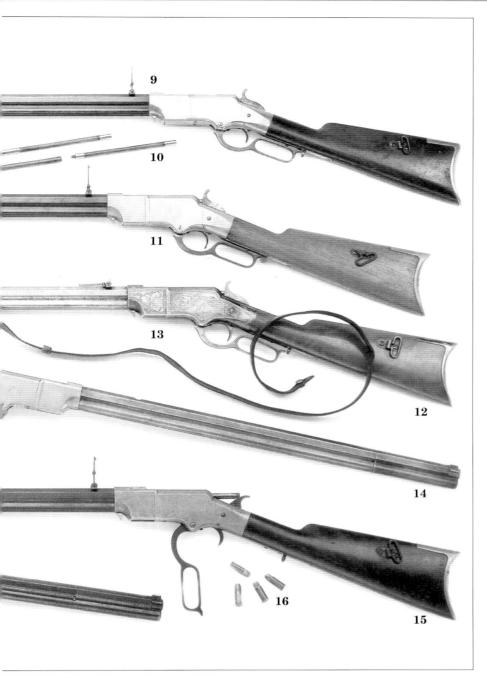

KEY:
1. *An early brass frame Henry rifle (s.n. 14).*
2. *Iron frame Henry rifle, levered for loading.*
3. *Iron frame Henry rifle (s.n. 155).*
4. *Early production (rounded butt) brass framed, engraved Henry rifle (s.n. 172).*
5. *Box of early .44 caliber Henry rimfire cartridges.*
6. *Early production brass frame, silver-plated Henry (s.n. 2115),*
7. *Box of post-Civil War .44 caliber Henry rimfire cartridges.*
8. *Early production brass frame, silver-plated, engraved Henry rifle.*
9. *Early production brass frame Henry military rifle (s.n. 2928).*
10. *Four-piece wooden cleaning rod stored in the butt trap of Henry rifles.*
11. *Later production (crescent butt) brass frame Henry military rifle (s.n. 6734).*
12. *Later production silver-plated Henry military rifle (s.n. 7001).*
13. *Leather sling for Henry military rifle.*
14. *Later production brass frame Henry military rifle (s.n. 9120).*
15. *Later production brass frame Henry military rifle (s.n. 12832).*
16. *Quartet of .44 caliber Henry flat-nosed cartridges.*

It is interesting to contemplate how much the Civil War would have been shortened if the Union had adopted and promoted the Henry and other breechloading rifles, of which at least single-shot versions would have been readily available. One Confederate general gave the opinion after the war that the South would have gone down after the first year, meaning that President Lincoln would have been succeeded by President Burnside or President Hooker. The Henry rifle would have been particularly effective in that the South did not have the technology to copy the weapon's mechanism or cartridge.

On the frontier, the Henry was equally effective. In 1865, two miners, former Union soldiers, drove off forty Blackfoot Indians. In 1866 Steve Venard, marshal of Nevada City, California, tracked down and, with his Henry rifle, killed three stagecoach robbers and recovered the considerable amount of money they had stolen, following which he received a reward of $3,000 and a new inscribed Henry.

Left: *Henry Model 1860, serial number 1, presented to Edwin M. Stanton, Lincoln's Secretary of War.*

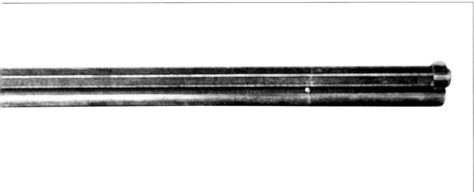

SPENCER RIFLES AND CARBINES

Of all the rifles and carbines (the latter having shorter barrels, for cavalry use) used by the more than three million soldiers in the Civil War, only two models were multi-shot repeaters, and one of these was the Spencer. Total Spencer production was about 135,000, as against only 14,000 for the Henry rifle. Both were highly effective, and it is tempting to wonder how much sooner the Union would have won if more had

been produced, especially since the South did not have the technology to copy these guns or their self-contained cartridges.

The Spencer used a tubular magazine inserted in the buttstock containing seven .52in caliber cartridges for Civil War models, and .50in for postwar models and conversions. The trigger guard acted as a lever; when depressed it rotated the block downward, extracting the used cartridge;

and then, when raised, a fresh cartridge was picked up from the magazine. The Spencer rifle was simpler and sturdier than the Henry and used a larger, more powerful cartridge. But it had a smaller magazine, 8 as against 15, and was slower to fire because the hammer had to be cocked separately from the lever action. The lever also acted as trigger guard. Downward pressure ejected the empty case (if any) in the cham-

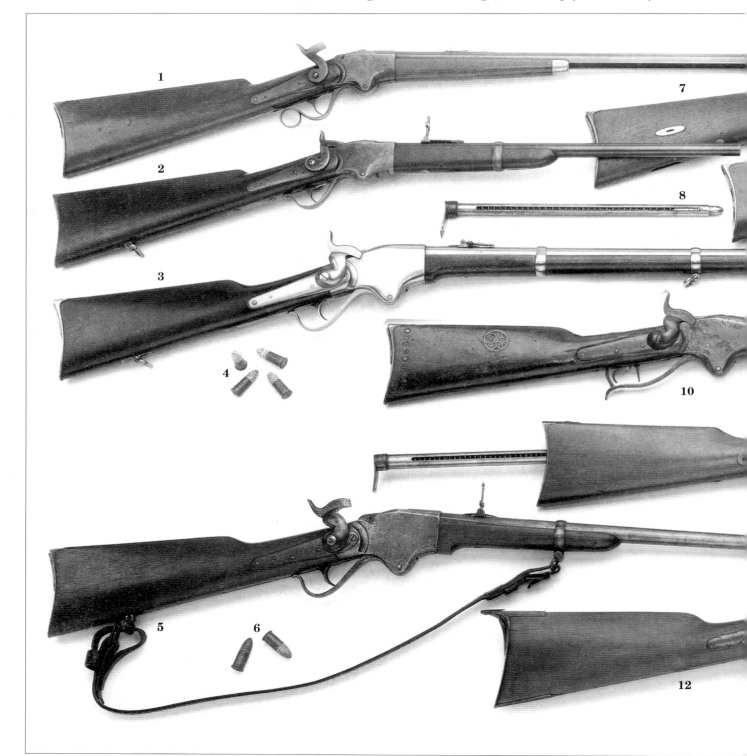

(Artifacts courtesy of Buffalo Bill Historical Center, Cody, Wyoming.)

ber and upward pressure loaded the next round, after which the external hammer had to be cocked in readiness for firing. It was a simple, reliable arm, cheap to make and sufficiently robust for service use. However, it was not adaptable to modern cartridges as was the Henry's successor, the Winchester.

With all its advantages, the inventor, Christopher Miner Spencer, a talented Connecticut engineer 27 years old at the beginning of the Civil War, had a difficult time having

KEY:

1. *Spencer .36 caliber light sporting rifle (s.n. 15).*
2. *Spencer .44 caliber light carbine (s.n. 5).*
3. *Spencer U.S. Navy contract .36-56 caliber military rifle (s.n. 121).*
4. *Four rounds of Spencer .56-52 caliber rimfire ammunition.*
5. *Spencer U.S Army Model 1865 .56-50 caliber military carbine (s.n. 5909).*
6. *Spencer .56-56 caliber rimfire cartridges.*
7. *Spencer .56-46 caliber sporting rifle (s.n. 17444).*
8. *Seven-round tubular magazine for Spencer rifles and carbines.*
9. *Spencer .38 caliber prototype sporting rifle (no s.n.).*
10. *Spencer .56-50 caliber carbine (s.n. obliterated), rebarreled to a sporting rifle.*
11. *Spencer .56-46 caliber sporting rifle (no s.n.).*
12. *Spencer .56-56 caliber carbine (s.n. 35862), rebarreled to .56-50 caliber by John Gemmer of St. Louis under S. Hawken's stamp.*
13. *Pair of typical Western saddle bags which might carry loose ammunition.*

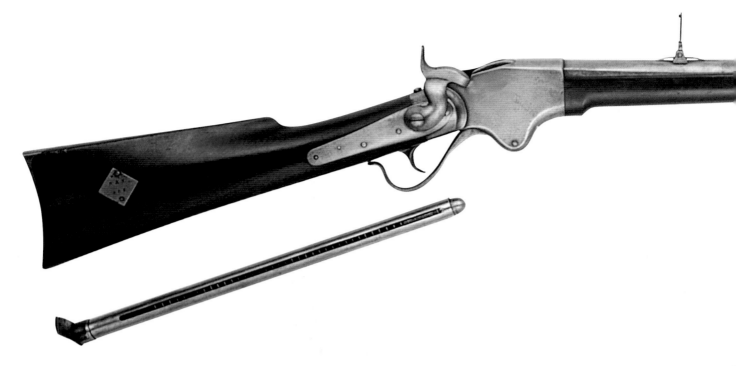

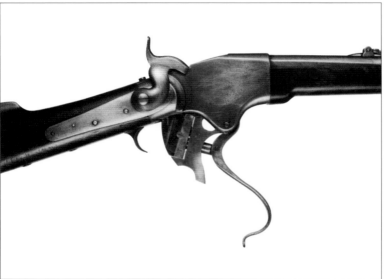

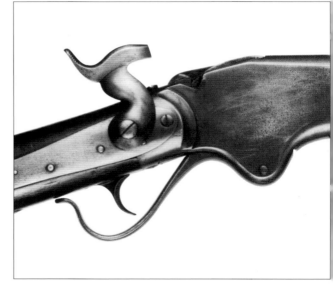

Top: *Spencer rifle, sporting version. The tubular object below the butt is the magazine, which was normally in the butt. The brass diamond is a museum mark.*

Above, left: *The breech mechanism shown in the loading position, The return of the lever would force the next round into the chamber.*

Above, right: *Breech closed and hammer cocked ready for firing. Sporting versions using more powerful cartridges were also made but were not popular.*

Right: *Spencer Model 1865 carbine, with the standard barrel, rather than the modified barrel which took the 0.50in caliber cartridge. The back sight has been raised for long-range shooting.*

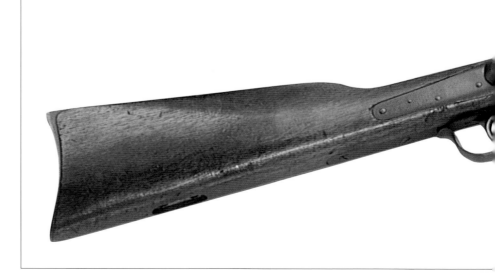

his design accepted. The Navy, circumventing the conservative Chief of Ordnance Ripley, placed a substantial order for itself and the Army in 1861, enabling Spencer to start a factory in Boston, in the former Chickering piano works. In 1873, when Ripley refused to allow the new rifles to be issued, President Lincoln interceded, after trying out the new gun in person behind the White House. Ripley was soon replaced and production proceeded, primarily of carbines for cavalry use.

By the end of the war the government had bought about 84,000 Spencer carbines and 12,000 rifles; this was quite apart from the many thousands previously purchased by individual States, regiments or persons. In order to speed the rate of fire still further, men carried pouches containing a dozen or so tubes of cartridges, allowing very rapid reloading.

One of the battles in which the Spencer played a crucial role was at Gettysburg, where Jeb Stuart's Confederate cavalry nearly succeeded in making an end run behind the Union lines, but was repulsed by George Armstrong Custer's Union cavalry armed with Spencers.

After the war a number of cavalry units in the West were issued refurbished Spencers, but these were replaced by the .45-70 single-shot Springfield carbines used by Custer's troops in their last stand at the Little Bighorn. Besides being slower to fire, the Springfield carbines had trouble extracting used cartridges, and there is considerable feeling that if the troops had been armed with Spencers (or Henrys, as well as the Gatling guns which Custer could have taken with him), the outcome would have been different.

Many Spencer carbines and rifles

found their way into private hands in the West after the war, but the Spencer Repeating Rifle Company found little demand for new arms. It was bought by the Fogerty Repeating Rifle Company, which had an unsuccessful prototype for a new rifle, and then Fogerty in turn was bought by Winchester in 1869, as one of a number of moves made by that company to eliminate competition.

There is confusion as to the caliber designation of the Spencer carbines and rifles. The Civil War Model used a cartridge officially known as the 56-52 and 56-50, referring to the measurements at the top and bottom of the copper case. Actually, the caliber of the bore was .52in. The postwar alterations by the Springfield Armory of about 11,000 carbines and 1,000 rifles were made by inserting sleeves in the barrels, reducing the caliber to .50in.

About 34,000 of the carbines were made under contract by another manufacturer, the Burnside Rifle Company, but only at the end of the Civil War. General Ripley having been relieved as head of the Ordnance Department, the Army finally realized how to promote the production of arms covered by private patents. There was a series of private companies that produced the Model 1861 rifle musket, the single-shot muzzleloading mainstay of the Union Army, but this design was actually developed by the Springfield Armory, not by a private company like Winchester and Colt's.

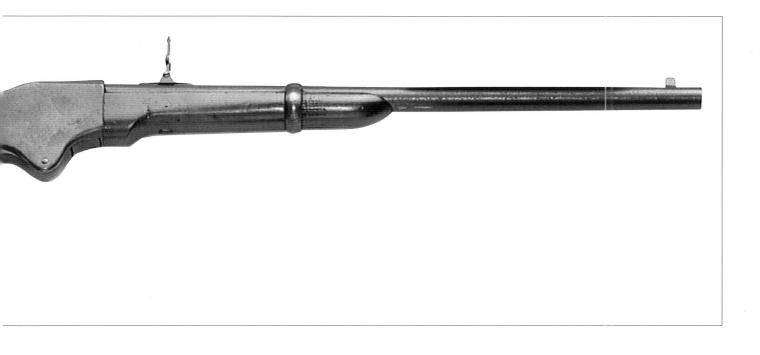

WINCHESTERS '66-'73

Just as B. Tyler Henry developed the rifle that bears his name, Nelson King, Winchester's plant superintendent, invented the improvement that produced the Model 1866 Winchester. This was a loading gate on the side of the receiver, allowing the cartridges to be loaded at the rear of the magazine instead of at the front. This also allowed the tubular magazine under the barrel to be completely enclosed, unlike in the Henry, and a wood forearm to be added.

Below: *Patent drawing of the Winchester Model 1866 rifle, with King's Improvement. Before this improvement, with the Henry rifle, the cartridges had to be loaded from the front of the magazine.*

Below, right: *Further patent drawing for the Model 1866, this time under the name of Oliver F. Winchester. The highly valued Nelson King stayed with the company until his retirement in 1875.*

While the same .44in rimfire cartridge was used, the rifle was more rugged and handier to use, and also was made in three styles with varying barrel lengths: the rifle, the carbine, and the military musket. The latter was not adopted by the U.S. Army as hoped, but nevertheless was sold in substantial quantities to foreign governments.

The Model 1866 retained the distinctive brass receiver that had been used for the Henry, apparently because Winchester had a number of these left over from the production of that rifle. This made the new rifle particularly popular with the Native Americans, who called it the "Yellow Boy."

The time was exactly right for the introduction of the new rifle in the West. The transcontinental railroad was under construction, cattle drives were being organized in Texas, gold and silver were being discovered in the Rocky Mountains, and there was

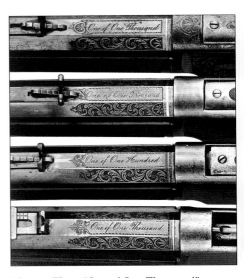

Above: *Three "One of One Thousand" Winchester Model 1873 rifles, and an even scarcer "One of One Hundred." The script and engraving are standardized.*

increasing friction between settlers and the Native Americans. Some observers credit the Model 1866 Winchester as the "Gun That Won

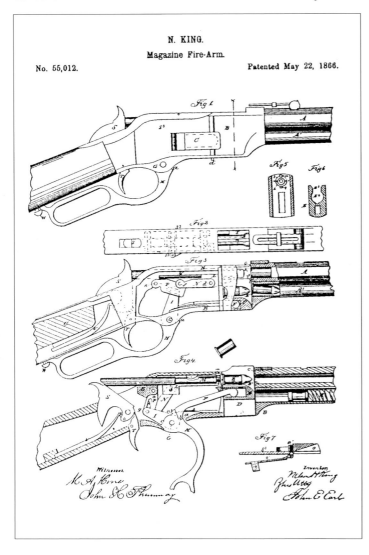

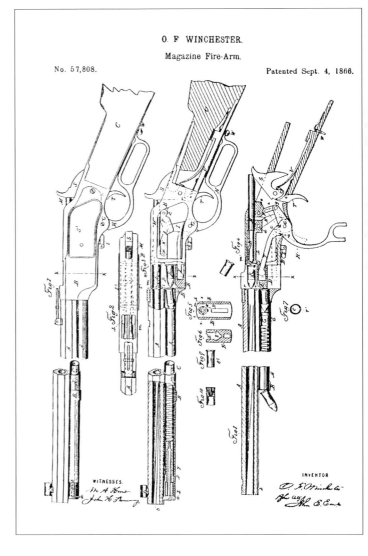

the West" instead of the Model 1873, which was introduced after much of the region's turbulent growth had taken place.

It was the Model 1866 rifle that put the Winchester Repeating Arms Company on a firm financial footing, helped also by large overseas sales such as to Turkey in its war with Russia. The company's dominance was assured by a series of purchases of competing companies as well as its patents on lever-action rifles. It was thus able to bring out the new rifle which is its best known as part of the history of the West, the 1873.

The '73 had a stronger and lighter steel frame and, most importantly, used the more powerful centerfire cartridge. For comparison, its .44-40 cartridge had 40 grains of black

powder, while the rimfire Henry cartridge had only 28. The centerfire cartridge could also be reloaded, while the rimfire cartridge could not, a significant advantage in the West.

The success of the Model 1873 is illustrated by the many calibers in which it was produced, from .44in down to .22in, and to its long period of production, all the way up to 1923. It has long been featured in Western movies, and was John Wayne's trademark. A popular movie in 1950 was "Winchester '73," with James Stewart. The centerpiece of the movie was a special version of the Model 1873 which was made by Winchester – the "1 of 1,000" in which each one of each of that number of rifles was selected for accuracy and given extra finish.

Above: *Texas Rangers Frontier Battalion, Company D, 1885. All are armed with the Winchester Model 1873, evidently ready for use. Apart from the firearm's intrinsic excellence, the timing was right for the Winchester to achieve success: the end of the Civil War had seen the beginning of a vast movement across the continent, and virtually every man concerned needed firearms for shooting game and for self-defense against bandits and native hostiles. Many of these men were ex-soldiers from both armies, and having seen the new repeater in action they would rarely settle for any other.*

Below: *Model 1873 in .44-40 caliber, bought in Texas and probably used for hunting buffalo by a railroad engineer.*

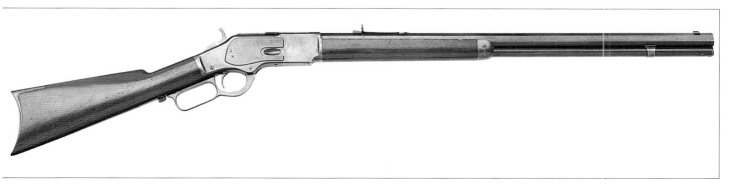

KEY:

1. *A fine Winchester Model 1866, .44 caliber, with 24-inch octagonal barrel and sling swivels.*
2. *Carbine version with a saddle ring and a round 20-inch barrel.*
3. *Some Model '66 rifles were made with round barrels on request.*
4. *Fine hand-carved leather scabbards were prized.*
5. *This Model 1866 was once Indian-owned – note the typical brass tack design.*
6. *Model 1866, with broken stock repaired with wet rawhide strips.*
7. *An original box of fifty .44-100 rifle cartridges.*
8. *Cleaning rod for the '73 shown in (17).*
9. *The cocking action of the Winchester – note how the breech-pin cocks the hammer as the lever drops.*
10. *Spent cartridges.*
11. *Some original "shells" for Winchester '73.*
12. *Two-part cleaning rod.*
13. *Typical 1873 carbine with the round barrel and saddle ring.*
14. *A '73 with a round barrel and fitted with a shortened magazine.*
15. *Fine '73 carbine.*
16. *Typical saddle scabbard for a Winchester rifle.*
17. *Fine example of the Winchester target rifle with additional sight set behind the hammer. This is a "peep" sight with Vernier fine adjustment.*

Above: *Model 1866 carbine, showing the saddle ring on the left side of the frame, and front and rear sling swivels. The saddle ring was included on most makes of civilian and military carbines through the 1800s.*

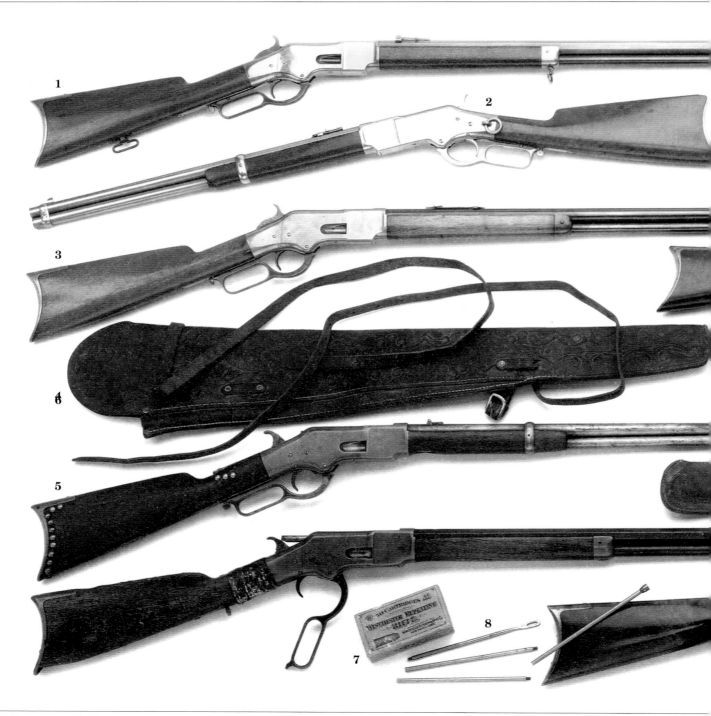

(Artifacts courtesy of Buffalo Bill Historical Center, Cody, Wyoming.)

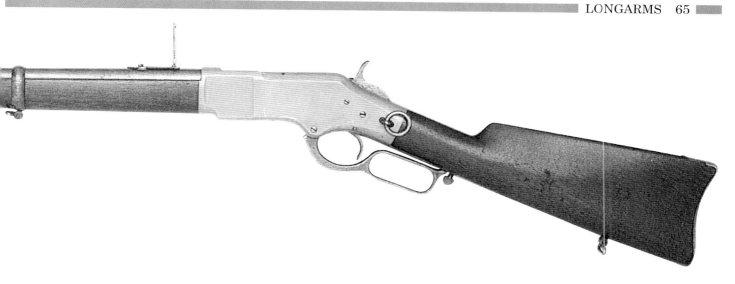

WINCHESTERS '76-'86

The Model 1873 rifle was prized for its large magazine capacity, fifteen cartridges in the magazine plus one in the chamber, and its rapid-fire capability, but it was not effective against big game or for military and other defense use in ranges over 150 yards. The Army had introduced the .45-70 cartridge, with a powder charge of 70 grains and a bullet weighing 405 grains which could be fired accurately at ranges up to 600 yards, while civilian single-shot rifles were using comparable cartridges.

To meet this market, and in a further attempt to win government contracts for military use, Winchester came out with a larger and stronger version of the Model 1873, called the Model 1876. Because of the limitations of the toggle-link mechanism, the cartridge it was designed to use – the .45-75 Winchester – did not have as large a bullet as the .45-70, but the powder charge was slightly larger. It was enthusiastically adopted by hunters such as Theodore Roosevelt, who used it to hunt grizzly bear, and also by the Royal Canadian Mounted Police, with whom it remained the their official rifle until 1914.

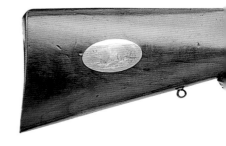

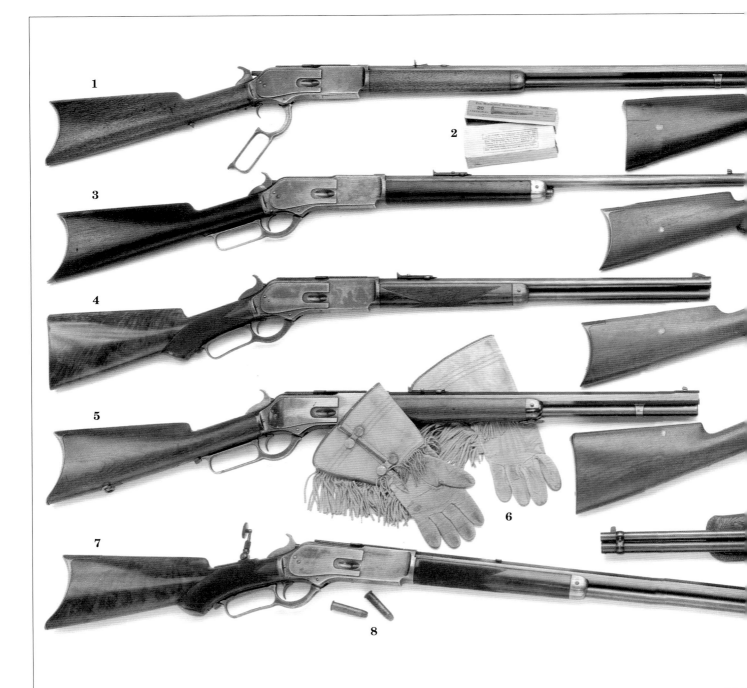

(Artifacts courtesy of Buffalo Bill Historical Center, Cody, Wyoming.)

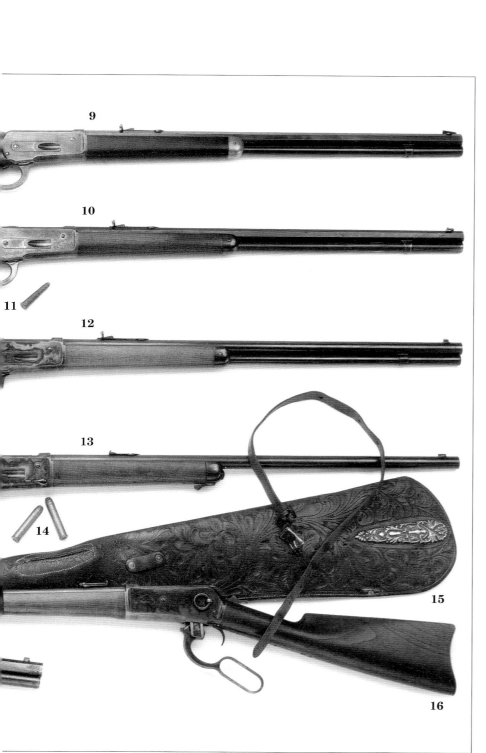

Left: *One of Theodore Roosevelt's special order Model 1876 carbines. Note half-round, half-octagonal barrel, pistol grip, deluxe checkered wood, case gardened receiver, half magazine, sling swivels, and shotgun butt.*

The new rifle was exhibited at the Philadelphia Centennial Exposition held in the summer of 1876, and is sometimes known as the "Centennial Model." Today it is impressive as a collector's item, with its extra length and heavy weight. However, the Model 1876 had limited production both because of its special purpose use and because the toggle-link mechanism joining the lever to the cartridge carrier, which had originated with the Henry, limited the size of the bullet.

KEY:

1. Superficially similar to the Model '73, the '76 had an enlarged receiver and bigger loading-slot plate.
2. Cartridges for the Model 1876.
3. Like the '73, some Model '76s were sold with short magazines.
4. Serial no. 45569 is a nice example of a Model 1876 carbine.
5. Serial no. 40330 in contrast is a fully blued rifle.
6. A fine pair of lady's buckskin gauntlets.
7. Serial no. 10018 is a '76 equipped with a checkered pistol stock and target sights.
8. Two .45-70 cartridges for the Model 1876.
9. The Browning-designed '86 rifle: big improvement on earlier models.
10. Similar weapon, with choice wood pistol stock and target sights.
11. Note long "shell" case.
12. "As new" carbine version of the Model 1886 (s.n. 84841).
13. The short magazine '86 rifle (s.n. 57909).
14. High-powered cartridges for the Model 1886.
15. Silver-embossed, hand-tooled rifle scabbard for the Model 1886.
16. Model '86 carbine with a ring which allows it to be slung over a saddle or shoulder.

Above: *Model 1886 deluxe sporting rifle, serial number 58102, in .38-56 W.C.F. caliber, with 26in octagonal barrel, with full magazine, varnished walnut pistol grip stock and fore-end.*

Above: *Model 1886 saddle ring carbine, serial number 59173, in .45-70 caliber, with 22in round barrel blued and case hardened, standard walnut stock and carbine-style butt.*

Above: *Another Model 1886 rifle, in plain finish with no extra decoration, half magazine with tang "peep" sight. The half magazine was for lighter weight for hunting.*

Above: *Model 1886 musket in .45 caliber with windgauge military rear sight. The musket was intended to compete with the Springfield .45-70 single-shot rifle which was the standard Army issue.*

Above: *Model 1886 lever action musket in .45-70 caliber, with 30in barrel with military windgauge rear sight. Winchester had hoped for military orders, but these did not arrive until the Model 1895.*

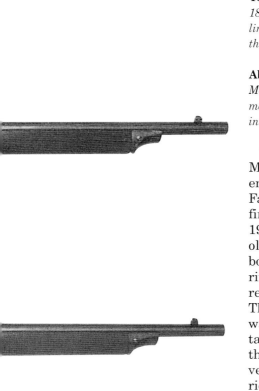

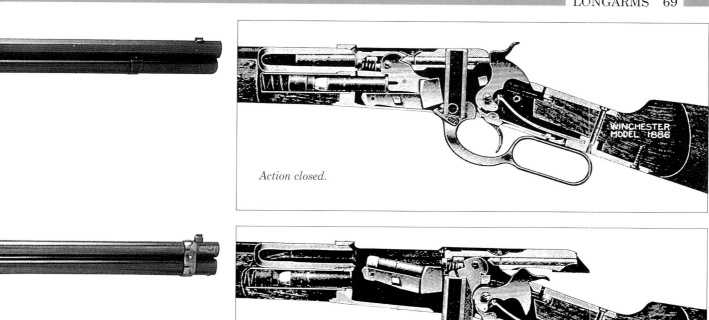

Action closed.

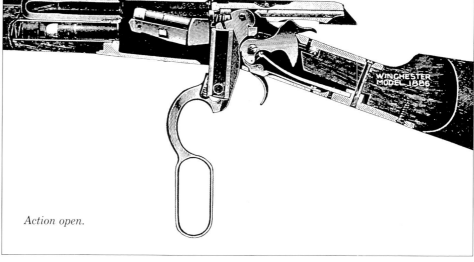

Action open.

Top: *Disassembly instructions for the Model 1886 rifle, showing the strong single vertical link which the lever operated, compared with the earlier toggle link mechanism.*

Above: *Instructions for assembly of the Model 1866, showing cartridges in the magazine and on the carrier, ready to be inserted in the chamber.*

This problem was overcome in the Model 1886, thanks to another talented inventor, John M. Browning. Famous as the world's most prolific firearms inventor up to his death in 1926, Browning was only 23 years old, in 1878, when Winchester bought his patent for a single-shot rifle and claimed the right of first refusal on subsequent inventions. The new feature in the Model 1886 was the replacement of the horizontal toggle-link system of connecting the lever, hammer, and carrier with a vertical action with twin locking bars riding in mortises cut in the side of the receiver walls and the bolt. This provided positive locking to accommodate high-powered cartridges. The receiver was shortened and streamlined.

The same basic design was used in all the subsequent Winchester models including the 1894, which is still in production today. The Model 1886 was one of Theodore Roosevelt's favorite Winchesters; he presented an engraved pair to the Metcalf brothers of Mississippi after the bear hunt that produced the legend of the Teddy Bear, and gave another to his expedition guide, Holt Collier.

The Teddy Bear story, as related in an exhibit at the National Rifle Association's museum, Fairfax, Virginia, is that on a hunt in 1902 in the vicinity of Roosevelt's Dakota Territory ranch, Roosevelt found a bear cub whose family was missing. TR arranged to save the cub and have it relocated to another bear family. The touching story found its way into the newspapers, who dubbed the cub the Teddy Bear.

The Model 1886 Winchester was still a black powder arm subject to emitting a cloud of smoke and fouling the gun's bore and action. It was not until the Model 1895, as described below, that Winchester designed a rifle to use the new smokeless powder.

THE WINCHESTER HERITAGE

A panoply of products of the Winchester Repeating Arms Company is shown here, from the Volcanic (the predecessor of Winchester) through the Model 1894 .30-.30 rifle which is still made today and is the most popular rifle among deer hunters. The use of the company's lever-action arms in the Old West has established a lasting tradition of dominance in this field.

While the lever-action handgun, the Volcanic, did not turn out to be practical in comparison with Colt's revolver, the Henry rifle combined a mechanical system which is largely still unchanged, with an esthetic appeal that is surprisingly modern. Here is a rifle, like its successors, which effectively combines form with function.

As described earlier, the Model 1866 "Yellow Boy" was similar to the Henry, down to its brass receiver, but with the major improvement of loading through the side of the receiver instead of the front of the barrel. It made Winchester's reputation in the West, and assured the company's success at the time.

The Model 1873 is the most famous firearm of the Old West era, together with the Colt Single Action Army, and both vie for the title of "The Gun That Won The West." It was made in many calibers and in large volume up to 1919 (total produced approximately 720,600), while the Model 1866 was also produced in large volume up to 1898 (approximately 170,100). A particular advantage of the Model 1873 was that its calibers

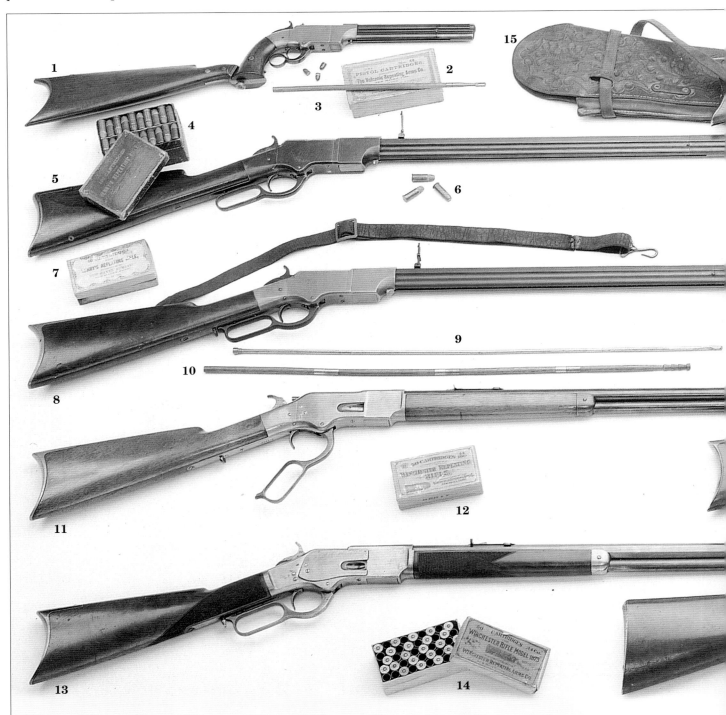

KEY:

1. Volcanic lever-action repeating carbine with detachable butt stock. The weapon is in .41 caliber.
2. Box of self-contained cartridges for Volcanic firearms, with three rounds.
3. Cleaning rod, very rare, for a Volcanic.
4. Fifty-round box of cartridges for Henry repeating rifle.
5. Early iron frame Henry rifle, .44 caliber rimfire.
6. .44 caliber flat-nose rimfire cartridges for Henry rifle.
7. Later fifty-round box of .44 Henry cartridges.
8. Brass farmed Henry rifle, as 5, above.
9. Metal and wood cleaning rod variations encountered with Henry rifles.
10. As 9.
11. Winchester Model 1866 repeating rifle. The brass frame is retained but King's patent loading port is obvious on right side of the arm.
12. Fifty-round box of ammunition for above rifle.
13. Winchester Model 1873 octagonal barrel rifle, most popular in the West.
14. Fifty-round box of .44-40 caliber ammunition for above rifle.
15. Leather saddle scabbard for a long-barreled rifle.
16. Winchester Model 1876 octagonal-barrel rifle.
17. .45-60 caliber round for above rifle.
18. Winchester Model 1886 rifle with shotgun-style butt.
19. Twenty-round box of ammunition for above rifle in ever popular .44-40 caliber.
20. Winchester Model 1894 round-barrel rifle.
21. Winchester Model 1895 rifle with tang rear sight.
22. .45 Winchester round for above rifle.
23. Leather ammunition belt with nickel buckle for heavy caliber ammunition.
24. Winchester Model 1887 experimental takedown shotgun. Its quickly detachable barrel assembly did not go into general production.
25. Twelve-gauge shotgun shell for Winchester lever-action repeating shotgun.
26. Mills patent shot cartridge belt.

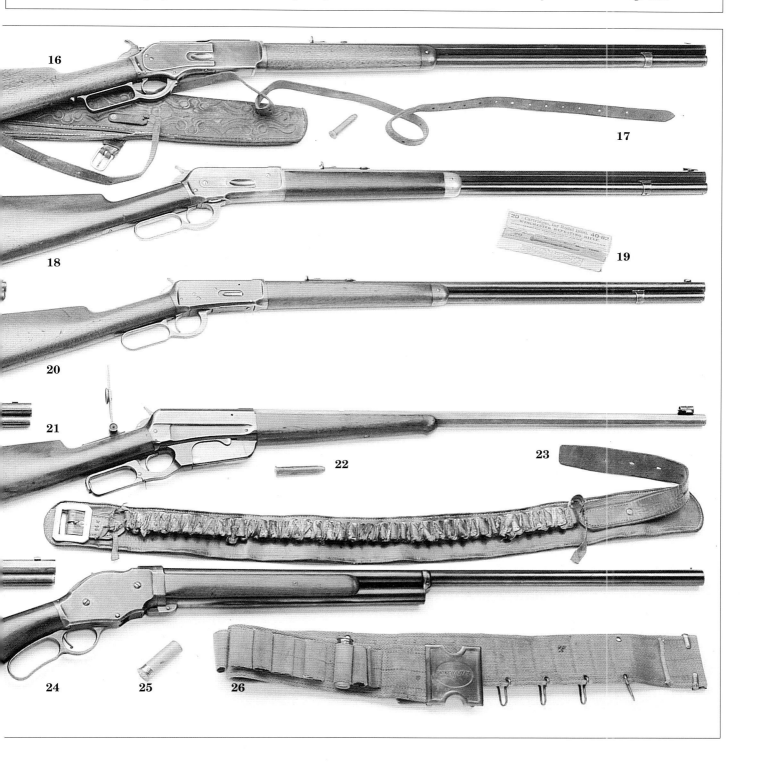

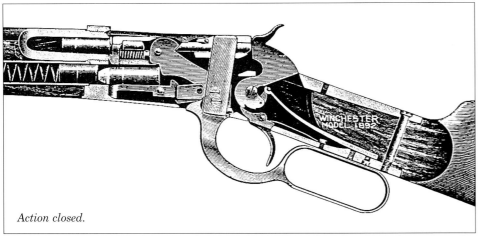

Action closed.

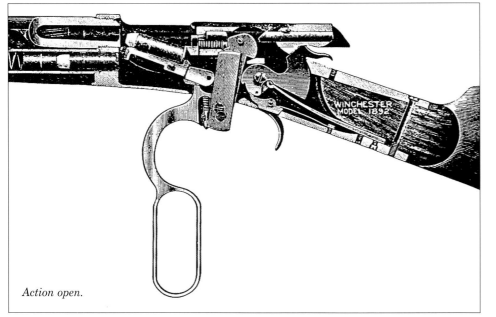

Action open.

Above: *Model 1866 rifle, serial number 107208, in .44in caliber. It has been deep relief engraved by the famous C. F. Ulrich.*

Left and below left: *Diagrams of the action of the Model 1892 rifle, as published in a contemporary Winchester catalog. The firearm was similar to that of the Model 1886, but more compact, adapted to taking lower powered cartridges for smaller game such as deer. It was a popular sporting weapon, with about a million made by 1941.*

not work with tubular magazines). It had considerable success as a big game hunting rifle, and was a favorite with Theodore Roosevelt. However, the rifle was not adopted by the U.S. Army, although a large number were sold to the Russians for use in World War I.

Philip Schreier, Curator of Programs at the NRA National Firearms Museum, has made a special study of Theodore Roosevelt and his firearms. He describes the Winchester Model 1895 and its relation to Roosevelt as follows:

"The 1895 Winchester was a departure from TR's standard taste in rifles. Designed by John Browning, the 1895 was the first Winchester to accept the new smokeless 'hi-powered' rounds that were now revolutionizing the shooting world. With a tubular magazine being not only impractical but dangerous as well when loaded with spitzer bullets, Browning developed a rifle action that still allowed the user to get off

matched those of the leading handguns, which were in .45in and .44in, so that the same cartridge could be used in both.

The Model 1876 was the first attempt at a rifle that could use large caliber, high-powered cartridges for hunting big game. It was replaced by the Model 1886 with John Browning's stronger action, and also the Models 1892 to 1894.

These were lighter, with a better grade of steel, and were the final step in the Winchester evolution (the Model 1894 was made for use with smokeless powder and is still manufactured today).

At the end of the Old West period, Winchester tried to adapt its lever-action rifle to military use, with its Model 1895 box magazine rifle (military cartridges with pointed tips do

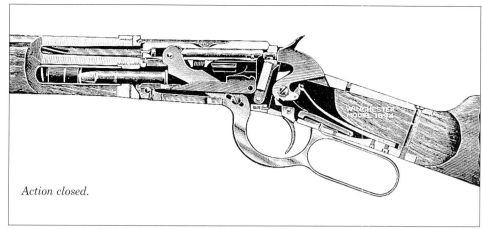

Action closed.

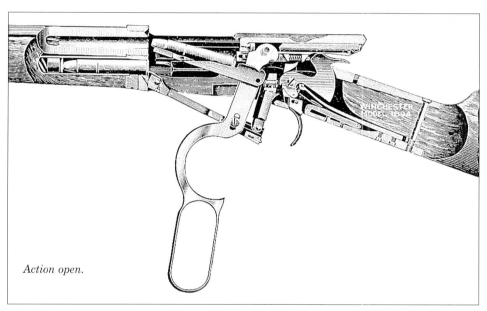

Action open.

quick successive shots that could hit harder and farther away with the new 'hi-power' rounds. Roosevelt had seen the awesome effect smokeless cartridges had on battlefield tactics in Cuba in 1898 when his men were subject to withering fire from Spanish forces armed with the new Mausers that used the smokeless powder. For Roosevelt, the combination of the fast working lever action and the power the new sporting cartridges packed made Winchester's 1895 the perfect rifle.

"Introduced in 1904, the .405 cartridge was the most powerful round ever developed for a Winchester lever action rifle. Roosevelt had to have not one, not two, but three 1895s in .405 and the firearm proved very effective on almost every sort of game in Africa. The big, 300-grain bullet was a hard hitter with an initial muzzle velocity of over 2,230 feet per second.

"In perhaps the best presidential endorsement of any product ever, Roosevelt wrote in Scribner's Magazine: 'The Winchester .405 is, at least for me personally, the medicine gun for lions.' He created a sensation for the gun that lasts to this day. The .405 was discontinued in 1936. However, rifles chambered in 'Teddies' caliber continue to bring a high premium over examples that are chambered in a round still readily available. In the year 2000, Winchester announced the re-introduction of the Browning 1895 in .405 caliber. The spirit of 'Big Medicine' is still alive and well."

Winchester also tried to adapt its lever action system to shotguns, with the Model 1887. However, it was a firearm that John Browning reluctantly agreed to design, and was rather awkward in appearance, with a massive receiver and a five-shot magazine under the barrel. It was made in 10 and 12 gauge, with 30in and 32in barrels, and also in riot gun form with a 20in barrel, but it had limited popularity.

Winchester also tried to adapt its lever-action system to shotguns, with the Model 1887. However, this was awkward, and the company replaced it with slide-action shotguns and, more recently, semiautomatic designs.

Above: *The diagrams show the action of the popular Model 1894 hunting rifle. The flat plate pivoting at the bottom of the breech distinguished it from earlier models..*

Below: *Winchester single-shot musket (2nd Model High Wall) built on an action by John Browning and introduced 1885: lever-operated, dropping-block, first of many Browning designs to be made by Winchester. Over 28 years' production, 109,327 of these elegant rifles were built in a variety of configurations and 59 calibers. Shown beneath the rifle is an original box of Winchester "Lesmoke" .22in cartridges.*

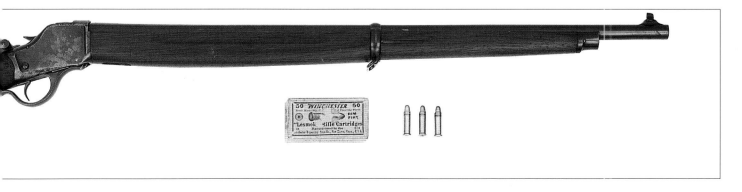

BURGESS-WHITNEY VARIANTS

Winchester had two significant competitors in the lever-action rifle field during the latter part of the Old West era, both located, like Winchester, in New Haven, Connecticut. The New England Yankee tradition of manufacturing ingenuity continued; there were no major gunmakers in the West itself after Hawken, although Freund & Brothers in Denver and Cheyenne were noted for their adaptation of the Sharps rifle.

The Whitney Arms Company had a long history going back to its founding by Eli Whitney, the inventor of the cotton gin in 1793. He was not able to profit, strangely, from that epochal invention, instead going into arms manufacturing, starting with a successful bid to produce 10,000 Model 1795 Army muskets. Under nephews and then his son after his death in 1825, the company continued to produce military and some civilian arms through the period of the Civil War. (It was the Eli Whitney's company that had produced Sam Colt's Walker pistols back in 1847).

Then, after producing a series of single-shot sporting rifles and military muskets that were sold in South and Central America, in 1878 the company joined with arms inventor Andrew Burgess to produce a lever-action rifle comparable to the Winchester. Also based on a patent by G. W. Morse, the rifle had a different operating system for the lever inside the receiver. Like the Winchester arms, the carbine version had a 20in barrel, while rifle had a 24in barrel. It was too heavy

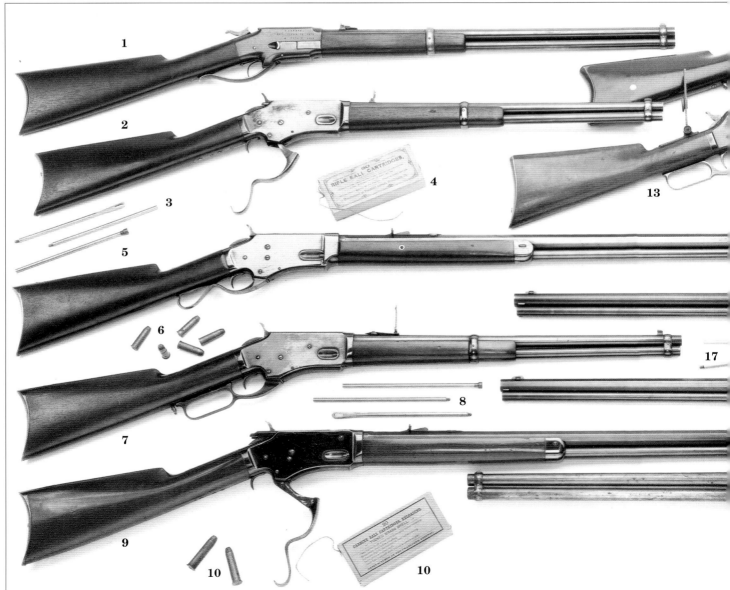

for sporting use, and was succeeded by the Whitney-Kennedy in 1879, which met with more acceptance (production about 15,000). One of these was reportedly owned by William H. Bonney, "Billy the Kid."

Finally the Whitney-Scharf was produced in 1886; it was a closer copy of the Winchester, but by that time Eli Whitney, Jr., had decided to retire from the arms business and sold the company to Winchester in 1888.

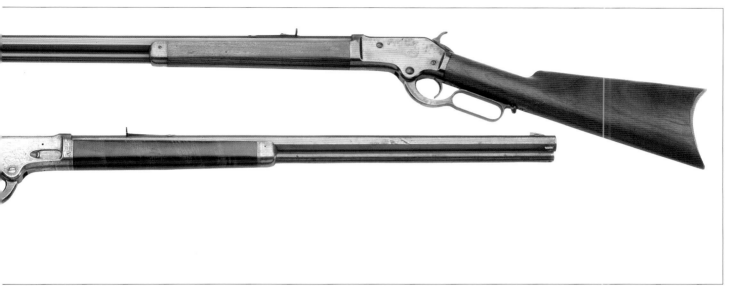

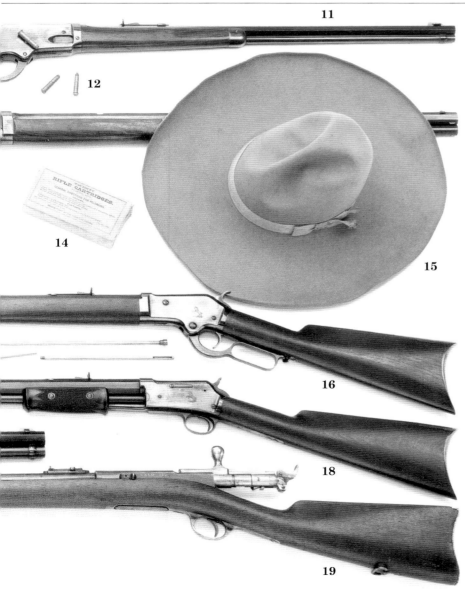

Above, top: *Colt Burgess lever-action rifle in .44in caliber. Fewer than 7,000 were made, production stopping in 1885 following a meeting between Colt and Winchester executives in 1884.*

Above, left: *Colt Burgess deluxe engraved, inlaid with gold, and inscribed from the Colt factory to "Buffalo Bill" Cody in 1883, when his Wild West show traveled to the east.*

KEY:
1. *Whitney-Burgess carbine in .40 caliber.*
2. *Whitney-Kennedy lever-action carbine showing the "S" lever on early models.*
3. *Three-part cleaning rod for the above carbine.*
4. *A box of .45 caliber "Rifle Cartridges."*
5. *A Whitney-Burgess Morse lever-action rifle in .44 caliber.*
6. *Ammunition for the above. Cartridges were called "shells" out West.*
7. *Whitney-Kennedy carbine fitted with a full loop lever.*
8. *Cleaning rod for the above weapon.*
9. *Whitney-Kennedy rifle in .40-60 caliber.*
10. *.40-60 cartridges for the above rifle.*
11. *Whitney-Scharf lever-action hunting rifle. It was sold in .32-20, .38-40 and .44-40 calibers.*
12. *Hunting rifle cartridges.*
13. *Another version of the sporting rifle.*
14. *Government "loads."*
15. *Typical Stetson type broad-brimmed hat.*
16. *Colt-Burgess lever-action rifle.*
17. *Cleaning rod for the Colt-Burgess rifle.*
18. *Colt Lightning slide-operated rifle. Colt produced a number of variants of this rifle.*
19. *Remington-Keene magazine bolt-action rifle in .45-79 caliber.*

LESSER-KNOWN LONGARMS

While most individuals in the Old West had mainly famous Colt and Winchester products in their personal arsenals, there was a ready market for lesser-known models and makes. The examples shown include a typical plain percussion shotgun, which was a common household item, for hunting birds and small game as well as for self-defense. Such a weapon was also often used by professional lawmen as well as outlaws, because of its effectiveness at short range even for inexpert gunmen. In the famous fight at the O.K. Corral, for example, Wyatt Earp's partner, "Doc" Holliday, reportedly carried a shotgun.

Fine shotguns as used by the aristocratic classes in England and the European continent for hunting birds as a sport were largely made there until the 1870s, when Colt and other American manufacturers began to produce equal quality shotguns. As referred to earlier, however, Colt did not stay in this field, because of the competition, and Winchester was not successful with a shotgun until its Model 1893 slide-action, designed by John Browning. Until the late 1800s, there was an overlap between muzzleloading percussion shotguns and breechloaders with self-contained shot shells.

The Roper revolving shotgun shown here is based on a patent taken out in 1866 by Sylvester H. Roper of Amherst, Massachusetts. It was first produced by Roper at Amherst in 1867, then in Hartford from 1869 to 1876. A revolving rifle was also made. The basic principle was the use of the reloadable steel cartridge cases. The number produced is not known. While apparently a viable idea, it is reported that the fragile mechanism tended to malfunction with hard usage.

The Marlin Firearms Company, founded in 1863 by John Mahlon Marlin, who had worked for Colt's, successfully introduced its first lever-action repeating rifle in 1881. Like Whitney, Marlin used some of the Burgess patents, but added features of its own. The rifle had an advantage over Winchester's Model 1886 in being able to handle large cartridges such as the Army's .45-70, and pro-

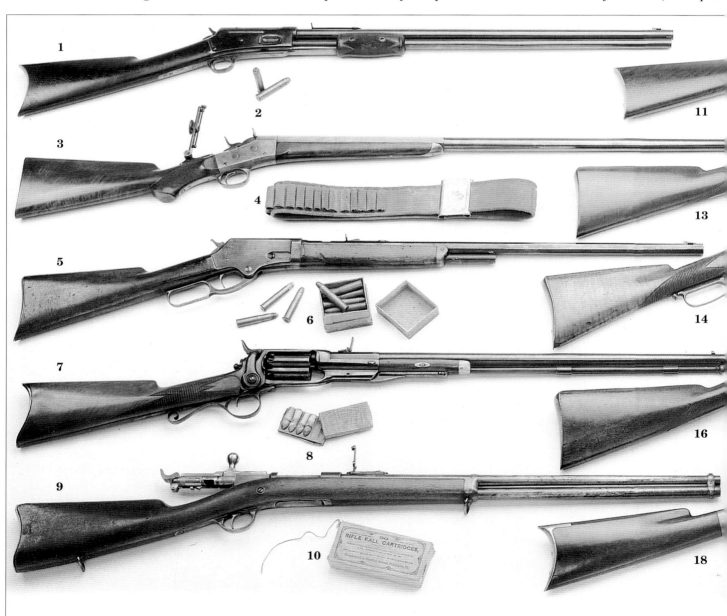

duction was over 20,000, in cartridge sizes ranging from the .32-40 to the .45-85. Next, with the help of inventor Lewis Hepburn, the Model 1888 was introduced, a lighter rifle designed for shorter length pistol cartridges. The Model 1889 made some improvements, and over 55,000 were produced.

Another successful Marlin sporting rifle was the Model 39A, which has been in continuous production since 1891. It was innovative in the 1890s, being the first rifle with a front-loading, tubular magazine, which could take 26 .22in Shot or 19 Long/Long Rifle rounds. The nose of the lever locked the bolt, while pulling the lever down and forwards would drive the bolt to the rear, over-riding and cocking the hammer, extracting and ejecting the spent case, and raising the cartridge lever, which elevated a new round from the magazine. Then, as the lever was closed, the new round would be chambered ready for firing.

The Remington-Keene rifle shown was made by Remington from 1880 to 1883, in a total quantity estimated at 5,000. It took the military .45-70 cartridge, and is known to have been issued to the Indian Police who were charged with maintaining order on Native American reservations. It was a practical alternative to the single-shot Springfield rife then in use by the military and was entered in Army trials, but the Ordnance Department was too conservative to consider such new development. Winchester's bolt-action Hotchkiss, with the magazine in the butt, had somewhat more success and was adopted by the Navy.

Bolt-action rifles were not popular in the Old West, because they could not be carried in saddle scabbards as could lever-action longarms.

KEY:

1. *Colt Lightning large frame slide-action rifle, competitor of the lever-action Winchester and Marlin arms, but never as popular.*
2. *Two .50-95 express caliber cartridges for the above rifle, the largest caliber available for this model.*
3. *Remington long range Creedmore rifle, once the property of General Custer and one of the finest Remington arms ever made; .44-100 caliber.*
4. *Mills patent type fabric cartridge belt with nickeled Winchester belt plate.*
5. *Marlin Model 1881 lever-action rifle with half magazine and octagonal barrel. Capable of handling large caliber ammunition, it was a serious competitor of the Winchester Model 1886 arms.*
6. *Box of .45-70 caliber cartridges of type used by the above rifle, a favorite caliber of hunters and soldiers.*
7. *Colt Model 1855 half stock percussion sporting rifle, made 1857-64. Revolving cylinder longarms were never entirely successful, always prone to mechanical failure.*
8. *Six-round packet of .44 caliber combustible cartridges for the above firearm.*
9. *Remington-Keene magazine bolt-action rifle. Popular with frontiersmen and issued by the U.S. Dept of the Interior to arm Indian Police.*
10. *Twenty-round pack of .45-70 caliber cartridges made at Frankfort Arsenal, Philadelphia.*
11. *Sharps Model 1874 sporting rifle with part octagonal and part round barrel, one of the most popular rifles of this company.*
12. *Twenty-round box of .40-70 caliber cartridges, one of the most popular calibers available in the above rifle.*
13. *Roper revolving shotgun, a 12-gauge four-shot weapon that utilized a reloadable steel cartridge case. The fragile mechanism tended to malfunction with hard usage.*
14. *Whitney-Kennedy lever-action repeating rifle. This arm appears to be a special order, as indicated by the fancy wood, checkered stock, and flip-up front sight.*
15. *Leather rifle cartridge belt with nickeled buckle used with appropriate large bore ammunition.*
16. *Unmarked, inexpensive, double-barreled percussion shotgun, 12-gauge, typical mid-19th century firearm.*
17. *Leather shot bag for use with any firearm similar to the above.*
18. *Ballard single-shot sporting rifle, made by the Brown Manufacturing Co.; a quality firearm.*
19. *Twenty-round box for .40-70 Ballard cartridges.*

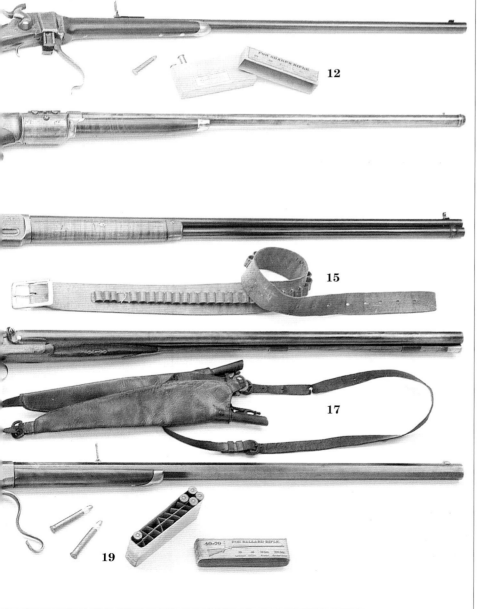

CARRYING LONGARMS

Any hunter, lawman, cowboy, or gunfighter carrying a rifle or shotgun would want his weapon to be protected from the elements and also to be easily to hand. At the same time, such weapons were heavy and bulky. A quality scabbard helped to protect the weapon and made it easier to carry.

Buckskin scabbards, often embellished with fringe or beading, could be easily made or purchased from Indians or traders. Sheathed in such covers, rifles could be carried across the pommel of the saddle, in hand and ready for use. By the 1870s leather scabbards, both plain and fancy, could be purchased from saddle and harness makers with buckles and straps to attach them to the saddle. Personal taste dictated which side of the horse the scabbard was attached to, and opinions differed as to whether the butt of the gun should face to the front or the back. Long-range rifles and sporting shotguns could be fitted to more rigid cases and boxes that could be stored or carried in wagons or other conveyances.

Out on the plains there lurked many dangers. Most gunfighters were more concerned with pistols than longarms, although many of them owned such weapons, and on occasion owed their lives to them. A pistol was fine for close-range shooting but of little use when confronted by hostile Indians whose ambition was to get up close. A rifle made sure they kept their distance.

The two Sharps cartridge rifles shown are typical of those used in the near extermination of the buffalo, but were also used for other game such as antelope and for defense against

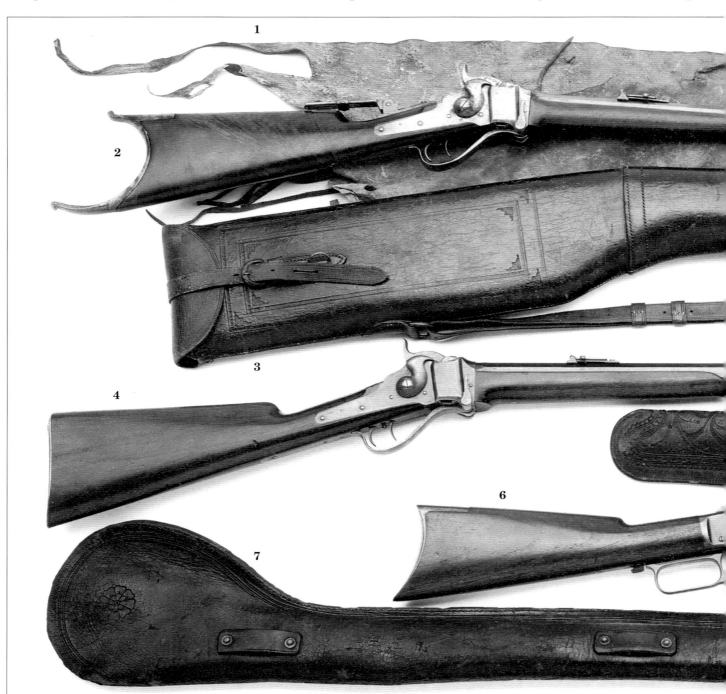

(Artifacts courtesy of Gene Autry Western Heritage Museum, Los Angeles, California.)

Native American attacks. From encounters such as at Adobe Walls in Texas, mentioned earlier, the Native Americans sometimes referred to the Sharps as the "Spirit Gun" or "Speaks Far Gun."

The fact that the Winchester Model 1873 rifle shown was probably used by a railroad locating engineer points up the role played by the transcontinental railroad, completed in 1868, and other later rail lines in the destruction of the buffalo and the opening up of the plains to settlement by ranchers and farmers. However, the Winchester '73 was used by all parties to hunt game for food.

KEY:
1. *Indian tanned antelope skin scabbard of about 1875, which was used by "Antelope" Ernst Bauman.*
2. *Sharps rifle used for market hunting by "Antelope" Ernst Bauman on the eastern plains of Colorado in the late 1870s.*
3. *Rare factory supplied leather case for the heavy 1874 Sharps buffalo rifle, made in 1877.*
4. *Typical 1874 Sharps hunting rifle, caliber .45, 27/8 in., made on special order from E. Z. C. Judson, better known as Ned Buntline, author of dime novels and promoter of the West.*
5. *Scabbard for a lever-action rifle of the 1880s or 1890s, made by F. A. Meanea, Cheyenne, Wyoming; there would have been an extra charge for the fine leather tooling.*
6. *Winchester Model 1873 rifle in .44-40 caliber, bought in Texas and probably used for hunting by a railroad locating engineer.*
7. *Standard rifle scabbard of about 1880 purchased for use with the above Winchester '73; a plain but serviceable weapon.*

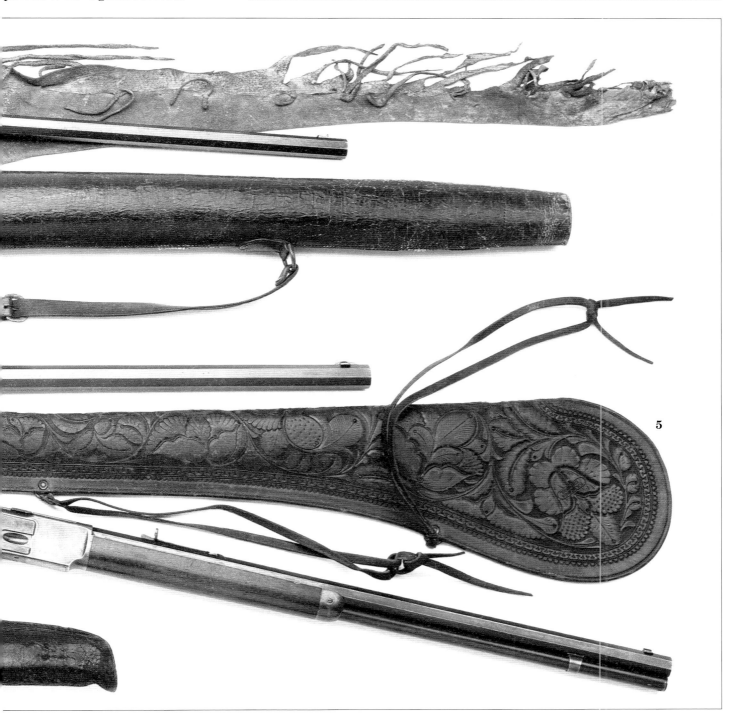

OUTLAW GUNS

A number of the handguns and longarms owned and used by famous figures of the Old West have survived and have been authenticated, although a number also have been inaccurately attributed to historic characters because of the collectors' value that can be added through such an association. Also, sometimes the historic figures themselves or their relatives traded on this value. "Wild Bill" Hickok was

reported to have handed out duplicate guns with notches he carved on the handles, and Jesse James's mother was said to have kept a bushel basket of guns she would sell to gullible tourists after Jesse was killed.

In any event, most Western outlaws owned various guns during their careers, and examples of these are a dramatic illustration of the use of Old West firearms. The Gene

Autry Western Heritage Museum in Los Angeles is a major repository of such examples.

Frank James's Remington revolver shown here is an interesting example of the diversity of firearms that were used in the Old West. Made

Right: *Frank James, who with his younger brother Jesse, and their cousins the Youngers, continued the life of robbery and violence begun with Quantrill during the Civil War.*

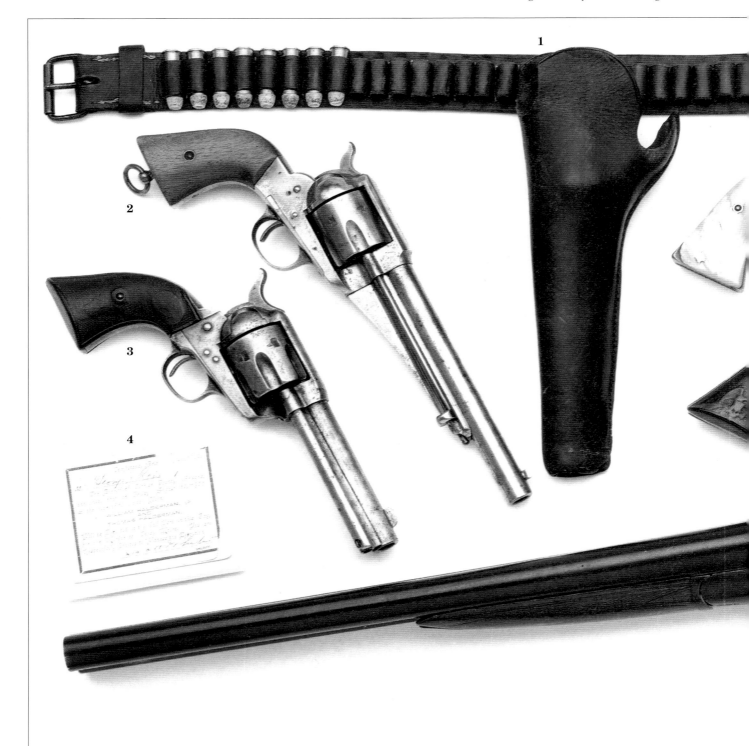

KEY:

1. *Leather cartridge belt with .44-40 cartridges worn by Frank James. The matching holster held the outlaw's Remington revolver.*
2. *Remington Model 1875 revolver, caliber .44-40, carried by Frank James.*
3. *Belle Starr's .45 caliber Colt Single Action Army revolver, carried by her near the end of her career.*
4. *Invitation to a hanging.*
5. *Colt Bisley, .44-40, which belonged to Pancho Villa, and was carried by General Jose Ruiz.*
6. *William "Bill Kick" Darley was a youngster when he joined the "Wild Bunch." Harvey Logan, better known as "Kid Curry," gave him this Colt .45 with nickel finish. Abrasions on the barrel are from twisting barbed wire around it.*
7. *This Wells Fargo wanted poster for Black Bart included descriptions of the outlaw and his various hold-ups.*
8. *Loomis IXL no. 15 shotgun with a short barrel. Charles Boles, alias C. E. Bolton, alias "Black Bart," carried it during numerous hold-ups of stages in California.*

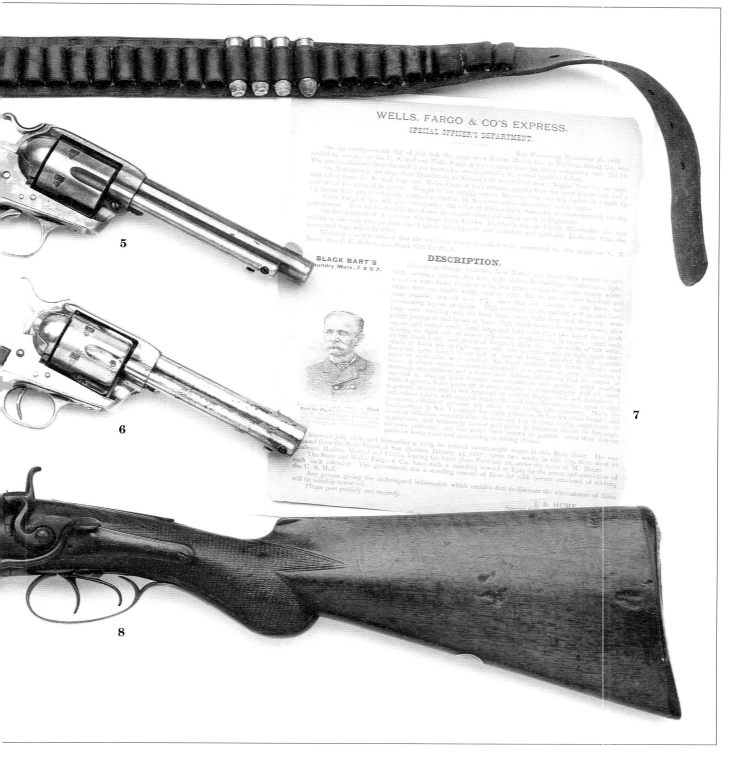

Left: *At the age of twenty-two, Jesse James was already a seasoned thug, having ridden with the guerrilla Quantrill toward the end of the Civil War. He and his older brother Frank later joined forces with their cousins, the Youngers. Jesse was shot down in his home in St. Joseph, Missouri, by Bob Ford on April 3, 1882.*

Below, far left: *Bob Ford was first sentenced to death for killing Jesse James, but later pardoned. He was shot dead by a James partisan years later.*

Below, left: *Robert Leroy Parker, alias "Butch Cassidy," at about the time he was in the Wyoming Penitentiary during the mid-1890s. There is no evidence that he ever killed anyone, despite his tough reputation and his life of crime. He is reported to have been killed by soldiers in Bolivia, but this and other stories of his demise have long been disputed.*

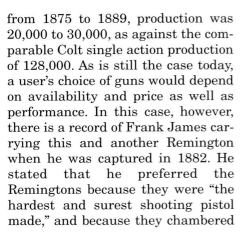

The Colt Bisley (the name comes from the English shooting range) was introduced in 1894, at the end of the time of the Old West, as a modification of the Single Action Army. The example shown was owned by Pancho Villa, the famous Mexican revolutionary who attacked Columbus, New Mexico, in 1916, was chased unsuccessfully by American troops under General Pershing, and then was pardoned by the Mexican government when his friends took power in 1920.

The nickel plated Colt Single Action Army revolver shown is associated with the "Wild Bunch," of Butch Cassidy and the Sundance Kid fame. Again, this was at the end of the Old West. From about 1895 to 1910, the gang operated out of the "Hole in the Wall" country in north central Wyoming, robbing banks and trains. The Union Pacific Railroad employed the Pinkerton Detective Agency to break up the gang, after which Butch and Sundance fled the country and may or may not have been killed in Bolivia.

Smith & Wesson revolvers were also popular with various outlaws. The First Model American top break revolver was the first .44in large caliber cartridge revolver to be introduced in the West, preceding the Colt .45in Army by three years. These were carried as well as Colts by Jesse and Frank James and by Cole Younger, who gave one of these pis-

from 1875 to 1889, production was 20,000 to 30,000, as against the comparable Colt single action production of 128,000. As is still the case today, a user's choice of guns would depend on availability and price as well as performance. In this case, however, there is a record of Frank James carrying this and another Remington when he was captured in 1882. He stated that he preferred the Remingtons because they were "the hardest and surest shooting pistol made," and because they chambered

the same cartridges as his Winchester rifle. He was captured shortly after his younger brother Jesse was killed by one of his own gang, Robert Ford, on April 3, 1882. Frank unaccountably was acquitted of robbery and murder charges, and died peacefully in 1915.

Belle Starr's .45in caliber Colt Single Action Army revolver was the type more often used by Old West outlaws. She was one of the few women known to have vied with men in their use of firearms.

tols to Belle Starr, the "Bandit Queen," who bore his illegitimate child.

When double action Smith & Wessons were introduced in 1880, it was understandably popular with Western gunfighters. It was preferred by William "Billy The Kid" Bonney, who owned a Smith & Wesson as well as a Colt; and later by the equally famous (at the time) killer John Wesley Hardin. The Smith & Wesson had the advantage of faster loading than the Colt since the barrel folded downward, exposing the cylinder and automatically ejecting the cartridges; but the Colt, with its solid frame, was sturdier.

The shotgun shown, an exterior hammer breechloading Loomis with a short (probably sawed off) barrel, was captured with "Black Bart" (Charles E. Bolton) in the late 1870s. He had robbed a series of stagecoaches, but there were apparently no injuries to anyone involved; he talked of unspecified injustices, such as by bankers, and was tracked down once his real name was known from laundry marks in his clothes left in San Francisco.

Left: *Harvey Logan in relaxed pose as he rolls a smoke. Known as "Kid Curry," he was considered to be one of the most dangerous members of the "Wild Bunch." He met his end in 1904 following an abortive train robbery.*

Below, far left: *Charles E. Bolton ("Black Bart") robbed stagecoaches, those of Wells Fargo in particular, during the late 1870s; he got fame for his alliterative nickname, and a long prison term for his inept robberies.*

Below, left: *The "Wild Bunch" dressed to kill – note the assortment of single- and double-breasted waistcoats or "vests" – but without a weapon in sight. Robert Leroy Parker ("Butch Cassidy") is the smiling figure to the right; Harry Longabaugh ("The Sundance Kid") is seated on the left.*

PAT GARRETT AND BILLY THE KID

The story of Billy the Kid and the sheriff who killed him, Pat Garrett, is probably the most romantic of all the tales of outlaws in the Old West. It is still shrouded in myth, and it is not surprising that there are few surviving firearms that can be attributed to either of these historic figures. However, more is known about the kinds of guns they used than the specific weapons.

Billy the Kid was born Henry McCarty in the Irish slums of New York in 1859. He migrated with his parents to Kansas and then to Santa Fe, after his father died and his mother remarried William H. Antrim. He fell in with bad company at the age of 15, and by the age of 17 was carrying a pistol and was arrested in Arizona for killing a man in an argument. Escaping back to New

Mexico, he joined and became a leading member of a band of gunmen hired by John Tunstall, an English rancher involved in fighting the "Lincoln County War" against merchant Lawrence Murphy and Sheriff William Brady. The range war ended inconclusively, after Tunstall was murdered by the Murphy supporters and Billy killed Sheriff Brady. After that Billy took to rustling, was

(Artifacts courtesy of Gene Autry Western Heritage Museum, Los Angeles, California.)

involved in another fatal shooting, and was indicted for murder, in the meantime becoming something of a hero in the national newspapers. Lawman Pat Garrett was sent to capture him, which he did, but Billy escaped, callously killing two of his guards. Finally, during the night of July 14-15, 1881, Garrett found and killed him, at age 22, in a darkened bedroom of a friend's house in Fort Sumner.

The Whitney-Kennedy carbine

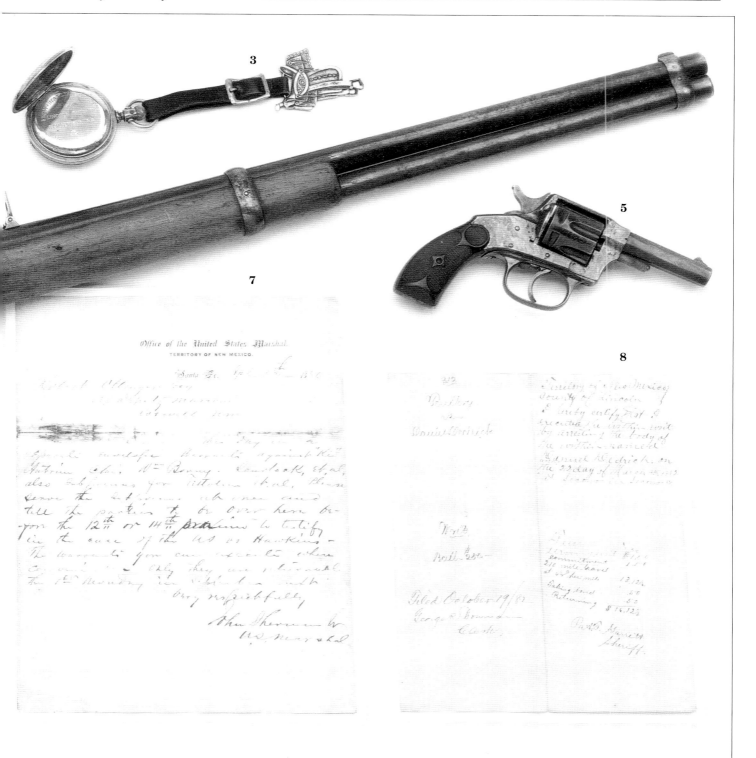

Above: *The Colt Thunderer was given such a name for appeal to the civilian market. In .41in caliber, it was a variation of the Model 1877 double action "Lightning." It was the kind of weapon Billy the Kid favored late in his very short "career."*

shown here is purported to have been presented by the Kid to deputy U.S. Marshal Eugene Van Patten for treating him fairly when in his charge. Van Patten treasured the gift, recalling the part he played in the Kid's life. This weapon was a model made from 1879 to 1886, much rarer than the Winchesters, which were in the most common use.

The two pistols shown are among several that were presented to Garrett by grateful citizens and friends after he finally ended Billy the Kid's career. They would not have been his normal sidearms, but reflect the interest in gun collecting which must have applied even in those early days.

Henry McCarty, alias William H. Bonney, alias Billy the Kid had lived and died by the gun. Indeed, it was the prevalence of firearms, and the general proficiency and willingness to use them that made young men like William Bonney so much a threat to the frontier community that in certain places like Lincoln County they could reduce civil order to a shambles.

Billy the Kid is known to have favored Winchester rifles and Colt revolvers, including a .44-40 Winchester Model 1873 carbine and a .44-40 Colt Single Action Army revolver which he carried when

Above: *Billy the Kid photographed in Fort Sumner in 1879 or 1880, about two years before he was shot dead by lawman Pat Garrett. This tintype correctly shows that the* Kid was not the left-handed gun he was frequently described as. One of his favorite weapons, apparently, was the .38in caliber Colt Lightning.

Garrett captured him for the first time. At his death, he had apparently traded this for a .41in caliber Thunderer double action Colt revolver. Following the Kid's first capture by Garrett, he seized his jailer's ten-bore Whitney shotgun, killed him with it, and kept it until his own death.

The gun used by Garrett to kill Billy the Kid was a.44-40 Colt Single Action Army revolver, of the same type that Billy had carried before his first capture.

The story of Billy The Kid is probably a good example of the relative unimportance of the gun duel in the Old West, contrary to movie lore. There is no record of Billy drawing his gun simultaneously with an opponent. The typical outlaw or lawman would try to "get the drop" on his adversary before he could draw; in the case of outlaws at least, they would probably set up an ambush. The shootout at the OK Corral was face to face, but at short range, not based on a duelist's countdown. An exception was "Wild Bill" Hickok, who engaged in his famous "walking duel" with Davis Tutt at 100 paces, in which Hickok shot Tutt through the heart.

This is not to say that outlaws and lawmen did not practice fast draws. Techniques for this were developed such as fanning, where the trigger was held down while the other hand worked the hammer, and slip-shooting, where again the trigger was held down and the hammer allowed to slip out from under the thumb of the same hand.

Above: *Pat Garrett caught up with the Kid on July 14, 1881, at Old Fort Sumner, in New Mexico Territory, and put two bullets into him in a darkened bedroom. Billy the Kid was already making a name for himself in the West and even in his native New York; the boy-killer's death turned him into a folk hero and a legend.*

JOHN WESLEY HARDIN

John Wesley Hardin was a hardened criminal who killed and served time for doing so. It is equally certain that lawman John Selman walked up to Hardin in an El Paso establishment – the Acme saloon – in August 1895 and shot him dead. There is also no doubt that Selman's sometime deputy and associate in petty crimes, George Scarborough, killed Selman in a darkened alley. On 6 April 1900, four years to the day that Selman was killed, George Scarborough himself died after being shot in the leg (it required amputation) during the pursuit of outlaws in Arizona. These three examples of violent people living in violent times help to contradict all too popular notions that the life of the lawman was a romantic part of the history of the West. Their guns prove testimony to the toughness of the times.

All the handguns shown are Colts; together with the Winchester, they illustrate the supremacy of these companies in the Old West. The two Single Action Armys, one owned by Hardin and the other by Selman, are of the model introduced in 1873 and still being made today. The pearl-gripped Thunderer and the smaller caliber Lightning were Colt's first venture into double action and were reasonably successful, although the mechanism was rather intricate and subject to malfunction. It is significant that both gunfighters Hardin and Billy the Kid carried these.

John Wesley Hardin presents something of a contradiction. He was certainly a cold-blooded and efficient killer, starting at age 15 during a visit to his uncle's plantation in Moscow, Texas, in 1868, when he shot and killed a former Negro slave after a wrestling match and then ambushed and killed three Union soldiers who had come to arrest him. His killings during his career, reported to total about twenty men, were

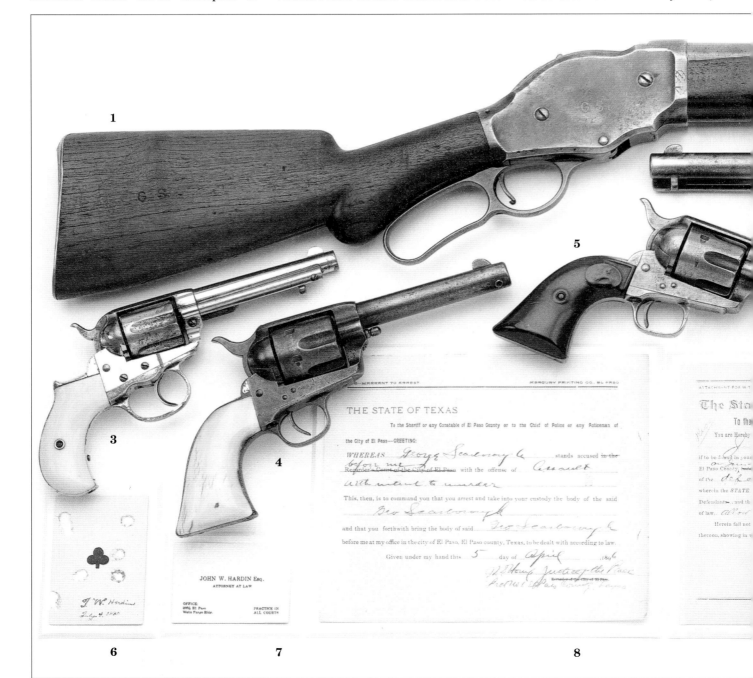

(Artifacts courtesy of Gene Autry Western Heritage Museum, Los Angeles, California.)

Left: *John Wesley Hardin, from a photograph believed circa the mid-1870s, wearing an arrogant expression suggesting that even in this relaxed moment the killer was ready for a fight!*

not primarily by face to face conflict, and he himself was shot in the back by George Selman. The other side of the contradiction was that he obtained a law degree by studying in prison, practiced law for a time, and had a wife (later a second) and children. Many of his descendants today proclaim themselves proud of their gunfighting ancestor.

Other guns owned by Hardin include a .36in caliber Navy Colt and an ivory-grip Smith & Wesson .44in

Russian model revolver.

Again, as with Billy The Kid, there was no evidence that Hardin engaged in face to face duels. Proficiency in firearms was evidently admired in the Old West, however, as evidenced by Hardin's trademark perforated playing cards. Back East, the sport of target shooting (Scheutzenfests) was popular, with elaborate German-style special target rifles. It is understandable that in the West there would be fascination with shooting the handgun, which was a common tool for self-defense and as a backup when encountering snakes, wild animals, bandits, and hostile Native Americans.

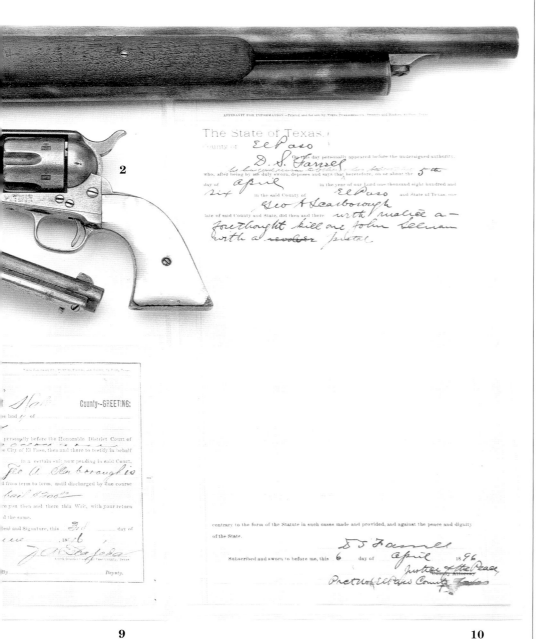

KEY:
1. *Winchester Model 1887 shotgun belonging to George Scarborough. "G S" stamped on the right side.*
2. *Colt with pearl grips carried by George Scarborough.*
3. *.41 caliber Colt Lightning which belonged to notorious Texas gunman John Wesley Hardin.*
4. *Hardin's Single Action Army Colt has had the ejector rod removed. The grips are ivory.*
5. *Lawman John Selman cut the barrel of his Colt .46 to 5in., making it easier to draw, hide, and carry.*
6. *Hardin demonstrated his shooting skills and gave away signed and perforated playing cards.*
7. *Teaching himself the law while in prison, Hardin could then hand out a different type of business card.*
8. *Warrant for the arrest of George Scarborough, dated 5 April 1896.*
9. *Warrant for the arrest of a witness to testify on behalf of the defense of Scarborough, 3 June 1896.*
10. *Statement dated 5 April 1896 charging that George Scarborough did "with malice afore-thought kill one John Selman with a pistol."*

DOOLIN, DALTON, AND EICHOFF

One of the last frontier areas to be settled was the "Indian Territory" that became Oklahoma. The government declared that, starting on April 22, 1889, settlers could enter the territory and buy land for homesteads at $1.25 per acre. This resulted in a huge rush that day, with some settlers sneaking across before the deadline (the "Sooners").

Until that time, law and order in the Territory was the responsibility of Judge Isaac Parker's court at Fort Smith, Arkansas. The Dalton brothers served for a time as deputy marshals until the oldest, Frank, was killed while making an arrest. The remaining brothers, Emmett, Grat, and Bob, became disillusioned and left to form the famous Dalton Gang of train and bank robbers. Their career lasted until 1892, when they were stopped by the local marshal and armed citizens in Coffeyville, Kansas, while trying to rob two banks. Only Emmett survived (after a term in jail, he became an advisor to Western movie-makers in California). The Colt Single Action Army revolver shown here is one of a group that Emmett claimed was used by the gang when they raided Coffeyville. If this is the case, the gang must have been relatively affluent, since the pistol is factory engraved with pearl grips.

William M. (Bill) Doolin was the leader of a gang of outlaws known as the "Oklahombres," which operated sometimes along with the Dalton Gang. He was killed by a posse in 1896. The Winchester Model 1886 rifle and Colt .41in double action revolver belonged to U.S. Deputy Marshal Louis Eichoff, who successfully tracked down the Doolin gang. It is interesting to note that he carried the latest available handgun, the Colt New Army in double action with a swingout cylinder, which was introduced in 1892. A latch released

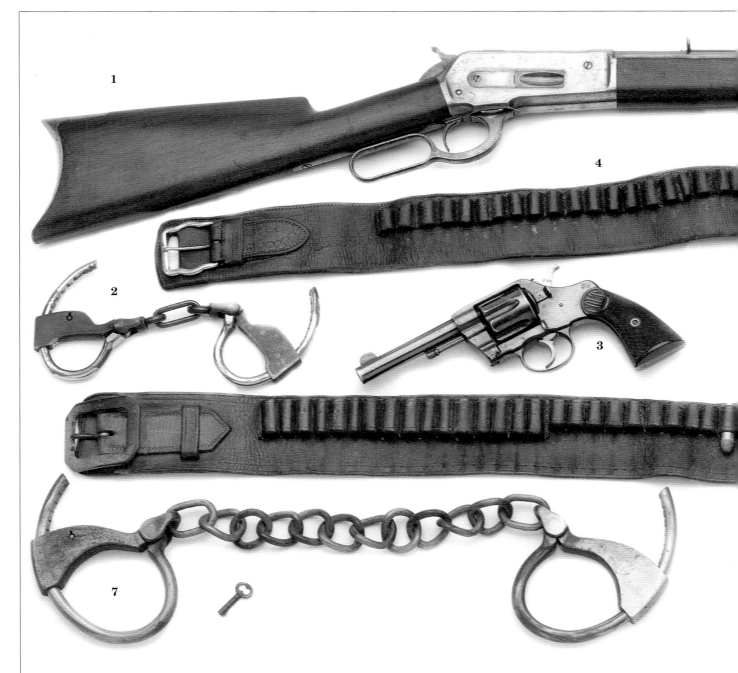

(Artifacts courtesy of Gene Autry Western Heritage Museum, Los Angeles, California.)

KEY:
1. *Winchester Model 1886, .40-82 caliber, carried in pursuit of Bill Doolin's gang by Louis Eichoff.*
2. *Handcuffs of the 1890s.*
3. *Colt Model 1889 Double Action .41 caliber revolver, which belonged to Eichoff.*
4. *Revolver holster and cartridge belt used to carry Eichoff's Colt .41.*
5. *Solid gold badge inscribed "To Louis Eichoff U.S. Deputy Marshal from C.M. [Chris Madsen]." (Madsen was a former soldier who resigned from the service in 1891 to take up a post of deputy U.S. marshal in Oklahoma.)*
6. *Leg irons and key used in pursuit of the Doolin gang by Louis Eichoff.*
7. *Shackles and key used by Eichoff.*
8. *Revolver holster and belt which belonged to Emmett Dalton.*
9. *One of ten factory engraved Colt .45s shipped to St. Louis from the factory with pearl grips. Emmett Dalton claimed that he and other members of the Dalton gang armed themselves with these guns when they tried to raid Coffeyville.*

Above: *Jennie Metcalf, or the "Rose of Cimarron," fondles a 5.5in barreled Colt Double Action Frontier Model. She was supposedly a member of the Doolin Gang of outlaws which had its hideout on the Cimarron River, not far from Guthrie, in lawless Oklahoma Terrirory, during the 1880s and early 1890s.*

the cylinder to swing out to the side, ejecting the used cartridges and allowing easy insertion of new ones. The Winchester Model 1886 rifle also incorporated a new improvement, the Browning action as described earlier.

The appeal of highly decorated arms is illustrated by the Daltons' purchase of Colt revolvers with factory engraving and pearl grips. Colt's made a point of this in their advertising, engaging top engravers like Gustave Young. The engravers had individual styles, some of which carry through even to the present, with engraving still available at Colt's Custom Shop at their factory located in West Hartford, Connecticut.

LAW AND ORDER

Establishing law and order was always a problem on the Western frontier, especially in boom towns such as San Francisco in the Gold Rush and the towns where the cattle drives terminated, and in remote areas where the government was not yet organized. However, records indicate that once towns became settled, crime rates were no greater than in the East. Face to face gunfights were rare, contrary to many Western movies, and most murders resulted from drunken brawls or family disputes. The accessories of the San Francisco vigilantes shown here are from the early 1850s, when the population of the city had grown too fast for the official lawmen. The vigilantes, organized committees of citizens, even adopted uniforms, and their equipment featured their motto of the "all seeing eye."

The first state to have its own police force was Texas, which founded the Texas Rangers at the time the state broke off from Mexico and became a republic, before joining the United States. The Rangers were disbanded at the time of the Civil War but reinstated in 1878. The Colt Single Action Army revolver was the standard issue, although not all were nickel plated and provided with pearl grips like the one shown. From his name, Tom Threepersons must have been a Native American.

The Colt Model 1861 Navy percussion pistol shown has "Wild Bill"

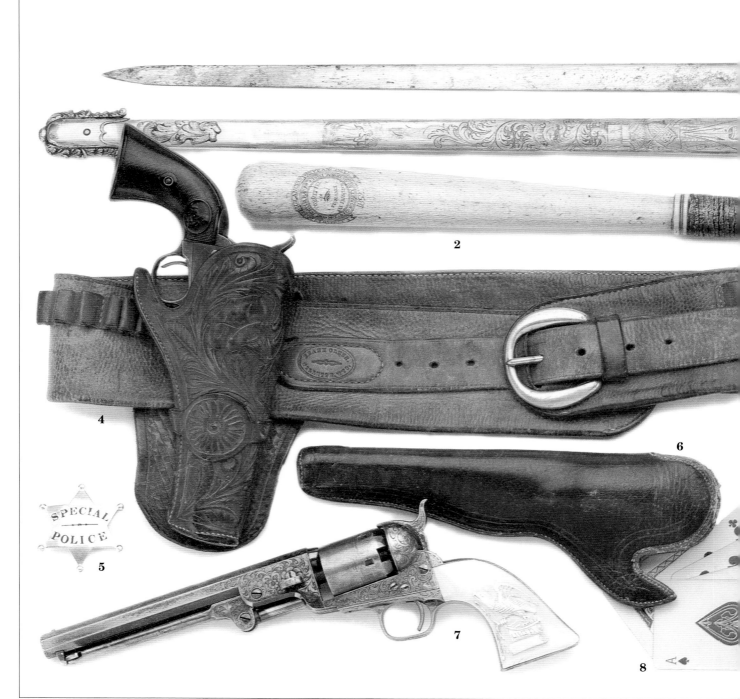

(Artifacts courtesy of Gene Autry Western Heritage Museum, Los Angeles, California.)

KEY:

1. San Francisco vigilante sword, silver plating, gold wash, precious stones, with the vigilante symbol of the "all seeing eye" engraved on the scabbard.
2. Ivory club carried by one Samuel P. Hill in the San Francisco vigilantes, dated 1852.
3. Silver pocket watch carried by Bartholomew Williamson. The silver fob has the "all seeing eye" of the San Francisco vigilantes – a different kind of badge indicating membership in the group. (Items 1, 2 and 3 from the Collection of Greg Martin.)
4. This holster, belt and Colt revolver belonged to George Gardiner, sometime cowboy, Wild West performer, and law officer in the 1890s and later.
5. Law badge worn by George Gardiner in Sheridan, Wyoming.
6. Plain, finely lined holster with the initials "JB" scratched on the back. Of the quality made by E. L. Gallatin in Cheyenne, Wyoming, the holster accompanies the Hickok Navy (7).
7. This factory engraved ivory Colt 1851 Navy bears Hickok's name on the backstrap. Serial No. 138813 chillingly reflects the "Aces and Eights" of his last poker hand. The actual pistol Hickok carried when he was killed was a Smith & Wesson Old Model Army, in .32in caliber.
8. "Aces and Eights" or "The Dead Man's Hand" held by Hickok when he was murdered by Jack McCall in Deadwood.
9. Colt Single Action Army .45 carried by Texas Ranger Tom Threepersons after the turn of the century.
10. Tom Threepersons' Texas Rangers badge.
11. Prohibition officer's badge, made from a silver dollar, and used by Tom Threepersons.
12. Sheriff's manual signed by successive sheriffs in Central City, Colorado, after 1882.
13. Reward notices for horse thieves.
14. Another source governing the activities of Colorado law officers – published Civil Procedure.

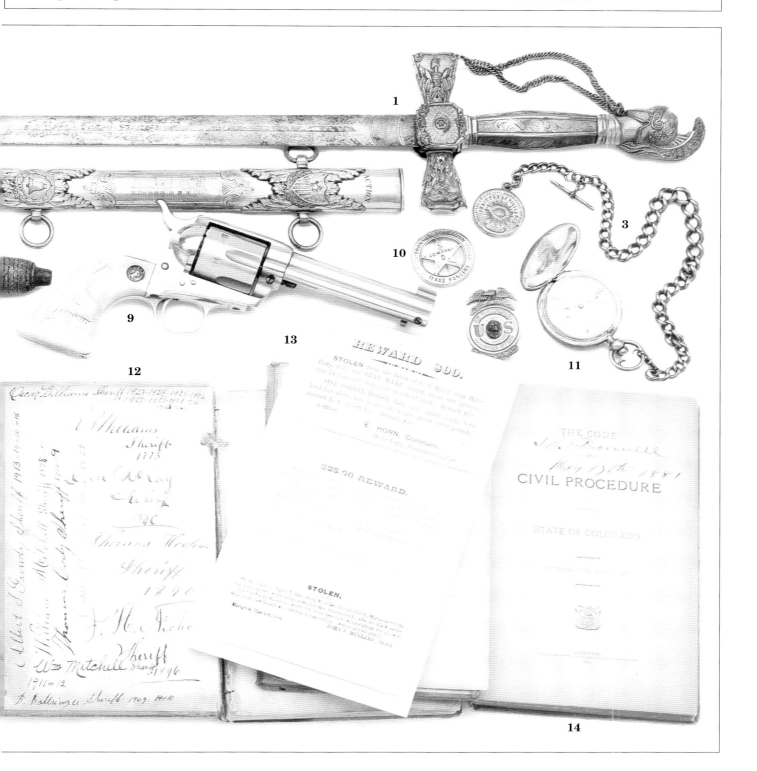

Left: *"Wild Bill" Hickok as he would have appeared in "Buffalo Bill" Cody's theatrical troupe in 1873.*

Above: *Bat Masterson was a well-known gambler, who nevertheless was regarded as law-abiding, which is as well since he served as county sheriff in Kansas and later as a deputy U.S. marshal.*

Below: *The Texas Rangers ruthlessly policed the southern plains Indians, notably Comanche and Kiowa, throughout the 1860s and 1870s.*

Above: *Texas Rangers initially favored the "Texas Paterson" Colt revolver, and later the Single Action Army, and Winchesters, as here.*

Hickok's name inscribed, but it is doubtful that this was actually his gun. He did carry a pair of this model when he was marshal of Abilene, Kansas. His title of "marshal" was usually applied to local police officers appointed by a town's governing body, while a sheriff would usually be an elected official , and usually at the county level. However, the terms were loosely applied and were sometimes interchangeable.

There were also U.S. marshals, appointed by the president with the approval of Congress, to enforce federal laws where local law was not available. The "Indian Territory," now part of Oklahoma, was a particularly lawless area, and a large number of U.S. deputies were sent out from Fort Smith, Arkansas, to apprehend wanted criminals operating there. A number of these lawmen, who received a bounty for their captures, were killed, while eighty-eight criminals were hanged outside the Fort Smith Courthouse.

Often lawmen in the Old West operated on both sides of the law or changed in and out of other occupations, but some were indeed dedicated officers of the law.

THE LAWMEN

Lawmen by any name – marshals, sheriffs, constables, peace officers – were tough and brutal men. Many had been on the other side of the law in earlier times or other locations. They were as violent as the element they were hired to control. Legend has inaccurately depicted, even distorted, these rugged frontier individuals. In early range wars, peace officers were often little more than hired assassins operating on instructions from the big game ranchers. Many were gamblers,

pimps, gunfighters and ex-convicts. They did their job because they could handle a gun, it was usually safer than rustling cattle, and they were paid well and regularly. Some among this group were loyal and honorable men but, as a rule, they were an unsavory lot. Regardless, the peace officer of the West was a colorful and feared, if not respected, man. As the frontier receded in the face of progress, so did the individuality of these larger than life men. And as it vanished, so did they.

Sheriff Wolf's Colt Single Action Army revolver shown here is a typical law officer's sidearm. It shows individuality in its ivory grips and also in the shortened barrel length, evidently so that it could be carried in a holster capable of a quick draw. On the other hand, Marshal Bunt's Colt has kept its long barrel as originally issued, in the same configuration as used by the U.S. Cavalry.

The engraved Colt Model 1851 Navy revolver with ivory grips is reminiscent of one of the most

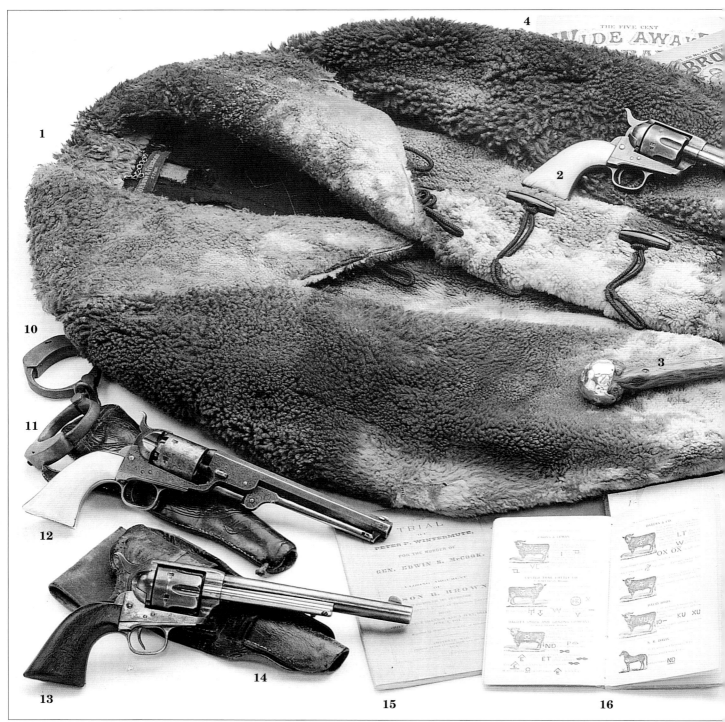

KEY:

1. *Wombat fur double-breasted overcoat worn by Henry Dahlem, first sheriff of Park County, Wyoming.*
2. *Colt Single Action Army revolver used by Sheriff E. N. Wolf of Lampasas, Texas, 1884-90. Wolf purchased the pistol in 1882 with a 7$^1/_2$in barrel and cut it off to 4$^5/_8$in.*
3. *Coin silver-headed cane engraved "Col. Cody 'Buffalo Bill' to Jack Stilwell, Nov. 14, 1893." The tip of the cane is a brass .40-44 shell casing.*
4-6. *Contemporary sensational pulp papers.*
7. *Nickeled iron handcuffs with key.*
8, 9. *Legal treatises: The Compiled Laws of Wyoming, 1876; Revised Statutes of Wyoming, 1887; Laws of Wyoming, 1869; and Session Laws of Wyoming Territory, 1879 and 1886.*
10. *Pair of metal handcuffs or restraints.*
11. *Colt Model 1851 Navy revolver, .36 caliber, percussion, engraved with ivory grips.*
12. *"Slim Jim" style leather holster for above revolver.*
13. *Colt Single Action Army revolver carried by Marshal William Bunt of Emporia, Kansas. Note 7$^1/_2$in barrel; .45 caliber.*
14. *Mexican double loop leather holster for revolver above.*
15. *Pamphlet: Trial of Peter P. Wintermute, Cheyenne, Wyoming, 1874.*
16. *Brand book of the Wyoming Stock Growers' Association, 1885.*
17. *Book: The Banditti of the Plains, or The Cattlemen's Invasion of Wyoming in 1892, by A. S. Mercer.*
18. *Five-pointed nickel silver badge of the Special Police of Livingstone, Montana, made by G. J. Mayer Company, Indianapolis, Indiana. (Courtesy of Old West Antiques, Cody, Wyoming.)*
19. *Pair of patent metal handcuffs.*
20. *Alligator hide traveling bag of Deputy Sheriff E. S. Hoops, Cody, Wyoming, c. 1890.*
21. *Dime novels of the period: Morrison's Sensational Series.*
22. *Pair of metal handcuffs or restraints.*

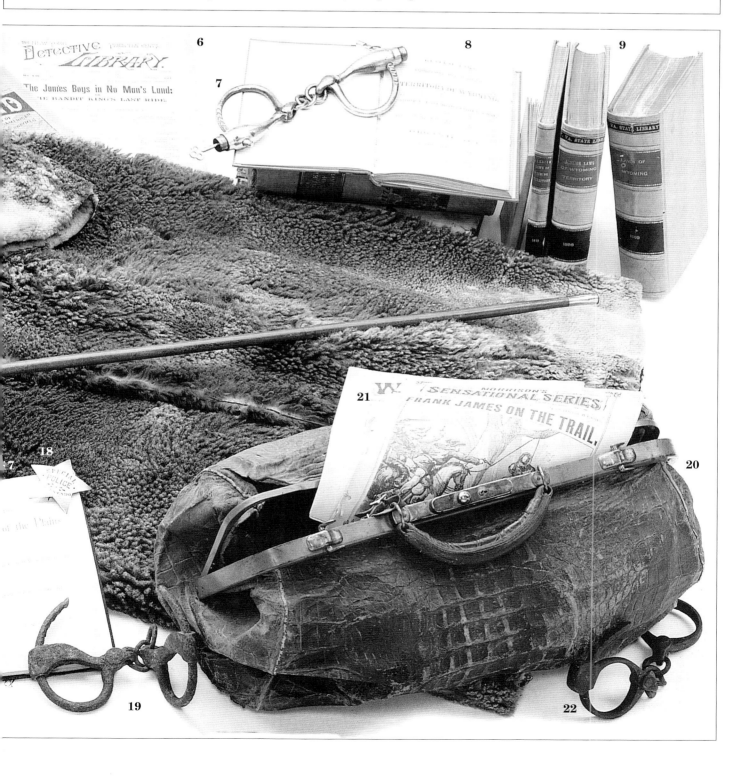

Above: *Arizona Rangers existed, too. Here Deputy Sheriff Farnsworth and (right) Ranger Foster pose well-armed in rugged Arizona Territory.*

Left: *"Wild Bill" Hickok was typical of a small number of men with dubious morals and violent pasts who nevertheless were hired or elected as lawmen in frontier towns because of their cool handling of firearms.*

famous lawmen of the Old West, James Butler "Wild Bill" Hickok, who carried two of this exact type when he was marshal of Abilene, Kansas, for eight months in 1871. He also used them in his famous "walking duel" with Davis K. Tutt in Springfield, Missouri, in 1865. This was one of the few actual examples in the Old West of face to face confrontations. Hickok shot Tutt through the heart, at a distance of 100 yards.

Hickok had a colorful career, spending as much or more time as saloonkeeper and gambler as he did a lawman and gunfighter. His reputation was first achieved in the killing of David McCanles in Rock Creek, Nebraska, in 1861, after which he served with the Union Army as a scout and spy during the Civil War. He received national publicity through the newspapers and

dime novels by the time he was appointed marshal of Abilene, which at the time was the terminal point of the cattle drives from Texas. He succeeded in gaining control of the riotous Texas cowboys, but lost his job after a gunfight outside a saloon where he accidentally killed one of his deputies (as well as the miscreant who started the fight). Later he toured briefly with Buffalo Bill's Wild West show, but was shot in the back and killed while in a gambling house in South Dakota.

One famous marshal who posterity considers was mainly on the side of law and order was former buffalo hunter William "Bill" Tilghman, who was also marshal in Dodge City and then in Oklahoma after the opening of the Indian Territory. Tilghman was called one of the "Three Guardsmen" in early Oklahoma; the other two were Henry Andrew ("Heck") Thomas and Chris Madsen, former Danish soldier and trooper with the U.S. Fifth Cavalry.

Perhaps a more typical story was of Dallas Stoudenmire, reputed to have served in the Confederate Army during the Civil War, and having received several severe wounds. After trying to make a living as a farmer in Texas he joined Company A of the Frontier Battalion of the Texas Rangers, acquiring a reputation for being able to kill without

compunction. After leaving to serve as marshal of Socoro, New Mexico, he was engaged as the marshal of El Paso, Texas, on April 11, 1881. Stoudenmire was well-known for his prowess with a gun; he apparently carried a pair of .44in caliber Smith & Wesson No. 3 "American" pistols, silver-plated and ivory-stocked, out of sight in specially made leather-lined hip pockets. He is said also to have carried a "belly gun," a .44in caliber Richards-Mason conversion of the Colt 1860 Army revolver, with the barrel cut down to about two inches.

Within days of his appointment, he took part in a gun battle between local citizens involved with bringing in Mexican cattle, in which he killed an innocent Mexican bystander and one of the disputants. By 1882 he had taken to drink, and was shot and killed while challenging one of the other side in the original dispute. Old-timers claimed that "it was alcohol that destroyed Dallas Stoudenmire. He was considered to be a man who, in his better moments, had deserved his good reputation."

The ivory stocked Colt .45 worn by Stoudenmire's original victim, George Campbell, is still owned by a member of his family. Its serial number is 22459, which means it was manufactured in 1875.

Above, left: *Benjamin ("Ben") Thompson, who earned a reputation as a gunfighter and gambler, and who served as city marshal of Austin, Texas, but whose past caught up with him when he was murdered on March 11, 1884, as part of a feud.*

Top: *John ("King") Fisher, former rustler, cowboy, rancher, and later lawman and gunfighter. He became a deputy sheriff, but was murdered with Ben Thompson in 1884.*

Above: *David ("Mysterious Dave") Mather photographed in Dodge City in 1883 wearing an "Assistant Marshal" band on his hat. He was said to have had links with outlaws in Arkansas, and had many of his own scrapes with the law.*

WYATT EARP

Wyatt Earp is revered by Western movie fans as the character played by Burt Lancaster in "Gunfight at the OK Corral." This famous event took place for real in Tombstone, Arizona, in 1881.

The town's romantic name, Tombstone, originated four years earlier when Edward Schieffelin went prospecting for silver in what was then Apache land. He was warned that all he would find would be his tombstone, but he made a major strike and gave the resulting boomtown its name, with a touch of irony.

Hollywood's most romantic, if inaccurate, depiction of Wyatt Earp's most famous episode is as a strictly "white hats" against "black hats" story with Wyatt (played by Burt Lancaster) as the leader and hero of the occasion. "Doc" Holliday (played by Kirk Douglas) is shown as wracked by tuberculosis, which actually was the case, and given to drinking and gambling.

In reality, of the Earp brothers, Virgil was the actual city marshal; Wyatt had been the marshal at Dodge City, and moved to Tombstone with his brothers because of its silver strike. He worked for a while as a shotgun messenger for Wells Fargo & Company and then as a County deputy sheriff, but had a business interest in two local saloons and a mine called the "Cooper Lode." As a Republican, he was trying to gather the votes to unseat the incumbent Democratic Sheriff Behan.

It was on October 26, 1881, that matters came to a head between, on the one hand, Wyatt Earp, his brothers Virgil and Morgan, and their friend Doc Holliday, and, on the other hand, Ike and Billy Clanton, and Frank and Tom McLaury.

The Clantons and McLaurys were part of the local rancher population,

Above: *Virgil Earp accompanied brothers Wyatt and James to the fledgling Tombstone boomtown in 1879. Once a stage driver and a deputy marshal in Arizona Territory, he hoped to find wealth in the silver-rich hills. He became a deputy U.S. marshal in Tombstone and swore in Wyatt and Morgan, together with Doc Holliday, as deputy city marshals for the gunfight at the OK Corral.*

Left: *Wyatt Earp may be regarded and depicted as a hero today, but in reality his reputation was not a wholesome one. He came to Tombstone in 1879 with a busy resumé: horse-thief, policeman, embezzler, assistant marshal, gambler – but always a considerable foe. His life after the OK Corral continued on similar lines; he died aged eighty in 1929.*

which resented outsiders brought in by the silver strike. However, their rustler activity was the talk of the territory; they had a contract to feed Apaches on a nearby reservation, but it was rumored that they had stolen the cattle from Mexico. At one point Billy Clanton stole a prized horse from Wyatt, whether by mistake or not, and the McLaurys were caught changing the brands on six Army mules which had disappeared from a local post. There were two Clanton brothers, their formidable father "old man Clanton" having died (unlike in the movie).

What led up to, and how the OK Corral actual gunfight began are still open to question, but there is no doubt that it took place between some pretty unsavory characters on both sides. Virgil had appointed his brothers and Holliday as deputy city marshals.

Attempts by the Earps to stop the

Above: *How Hollywood has depicted the famous gunfight at the OK Corral: the Earps are led by Wyatt (Burt Lancaster), second from left, while Doc Holliday, played by Kirk Douglas, is shown at left. In reality, in dress and manner, the Earps exemplified the typical gunfighter: wide-brimmed, low-crowned black hats and long "Prince Albert" frock coats. Wyatt carried a .44in Smith & Wesson New Model No. 3 "American," while his brothers and Holliday carried .45 Colt Peacemakers. Holliday also had a shotgun.*

rustling activities of the Clantons and McLaurys, and a series of personal confrontations, led to the Earps being notified that the opposing party was waiting for them at the OK Corral for a showdown. Ignoring the pleas of County Sheriff Behan to disarm themselves, the three Earps and Holliday set out for the corral.

Contrary to the movie, the actual gunfight was of short duration and at close range. Its story is worth retelling as a premier example of the use of Old West guns in a clash between lawmen and outlaws.

The two groups confronted each

other only eight feet apart, on open ground in front of the corral. Wyatt Earp later claimed that Sheriff Behan had told them the other party was disarmed, but that he saw pistols in the hands of two of them. He maintained that Virgil first ordered them to give up their guns, but that Billy Clanton and Frank McLaury went for their pistols, and that he (Wyatt) then opened fire. Wyatt's first shot hit Frank McLaury, but the latter managed to get one shot off before staggering off toward the street. Ike ran, Morgan shot Billy Clanton, and Holliday shot Tom McLaury, who tried to hide behind Frank McLaury's terrified horse, having dragged his brother's Winchester from its saddle scabbard. Morgan, meanwhile, had managed to put a pistol ball into Billy Clanton's right wrist and another in his chest. The boy staggered back against what was known as Fly's Gallery, and tried desperately to use his pistol with his good hand. At that moment, Frank's horse bolted, exposing Tom McLaury to Holliday, who fired his second barrel into him, almost knocking him off

Top *Wyatt's younger brother Morgan was normally a "pleasant outgoing" man, but under stress was inclined to be hot-headed. He survived the gunfight at the OK Corral, only to be gunned down in a saloon in 1882.*

Above: *John "Doc" Holliday and Wyatt Earp had met in Dodge City. Holliday had all the right attributes for the friendship: gambler, sometime dentist, alcoholic, consumptive, he was also a cold-hearted killer. He died from his illness on November 8, 1887, at the age of thirty-six.*

his feet. As his waistcoat became bloodied, Tom screamed in great agony, staggered into Fremont Street, and died.

Virgil, surprisingly, had not yet fired a shot, but he received a ball in the calf of his leg, which knocked him to the ground. Frank McLaury raised himself up and fired at Doc Holliday, who had tossed aside his shotgun and pulled his nickel-plated six-shooter. Both men fired together. Doc missed, but Frank's shot nicked Doc's hip, removing a piece of skin and a part of his pistol holster.

Morgan, too, had problems. Billy

(Artifacts courtesy of Gene Autry Western Heritage Museum, Los Angeles, California.)

Clanton, with his last shot, managed to put a ball in his shoulder, and was promptly shot by Wyatt.

The fight actually lasted only about thirty seconds, and an estimated seventeen shots were fired. At the end, three of the eight men involved were dead, three were badly wounded, and only two – Wyatt Earp and Ike Clanton – escaped without a scratch. Sheriff Behan and Ike Clanton swore out a warrant for the arrest of the Earps for murder, but the court found insufficient evidence to proceed with a charge of murder

against the Earps and Holliday, and they were released.

Information was recorded showing that the Clantons and the McLaurys used Colt Single Action Armys and that Wyatt Earp carried a Smith & Wesson New Model American revolver. The actual guns used in the fight have disappeared, but the Colt Armys and the breechloading shotgun shown here are representative of those that would have been present. The last item shown, a long-barreled "Buntline" Colt pistol, is not. Wyatt Earp's biographer Stuart

Lake invented the myth in 1929 that Ned Buntline, a dime novel writer, gave such a gun to Earp in 1876. The Colt company made a few of this model over the years, but not for Buntline nor for Wyatt Earp.

The aftermath of the fight continued the violence. Morgan Earp was murdered in a saloon and Virgil was maimed by a shotgun blast. Then Wyatt killed one of the presumed murderers and an associate of the second. It is reported that there was relief in Arizona and nationwide when the remaining Earps left the

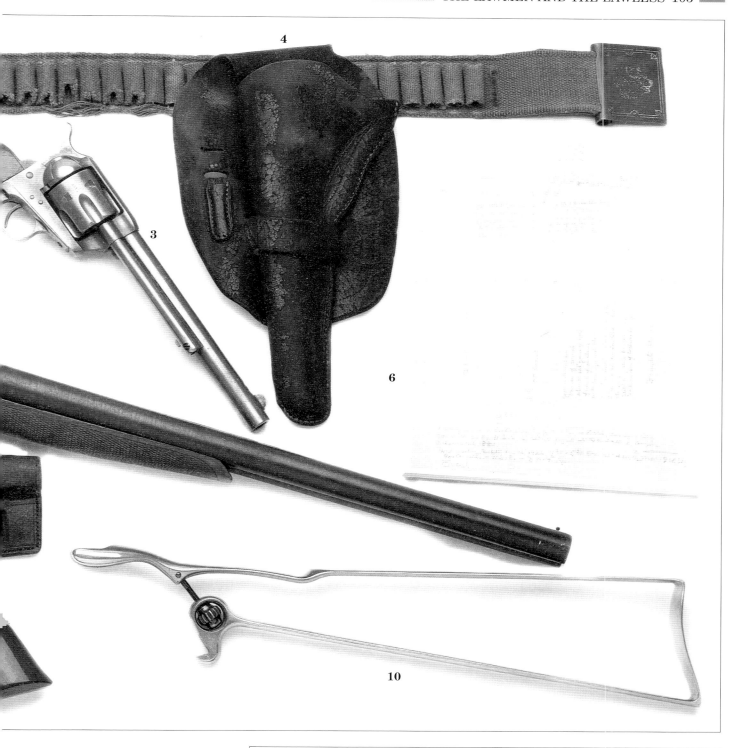

state. Wyatt settled in California, engaged in real estate, and died peacefully in 1929, a symbol of the end of the Old West with its tradition of the gun.

A highlight of the Gene Autry Museum of Western Heritage located in Griffith Park in Los Angeles, California, is a full-scale diorama of the famous gunfight, complete with sound effects. Examples of types of guns used are shown, together with many other Western arms. There is also a small movie theater, showing examples of how Hollywood has treated this famous event.

KEY:
1. *Colt Single Action .45 used by Doc Holliday. He told his nephew he carried this throughout his Western adventures.*
2. *Colt Single Action .45 used by Wells Fargo detective Fred Dodge who claimed that Wyatt Earp borrowed the gun at the time Curly Bill Brocius was killed.*
3. *Colt Single Action .44-40 used by John Clum while editor of the Tombstone* Epitaph *and during the capture of Geronimo.*
4. *Holster for Clum's Colt, purchased by him at Spangenburg gunsmith shop in Tombstone.*
5. *Web cartridge belt used by John Clum.*
6. *Diagram of Tombstone gunfight drawn by Wyatt Earp in later years.*
7. *Double-barrel shotgun reportedly used by Wyatt Earp to kill Frank Stilwell, one of the killers of Morgan Earp.*
8. *Factory holster for a long-barrel Colt Single Action.*
9. *Colt Single Action .45 with extra long 16in barrel and adjustable rear sight.*
10. *Detachable shoulder stock for the long-barrel Colt, used to convert the handgun into a handy carbine.*

RIDING SHOTGUN

The stagecoach was a vital means of transportation in the Old West, even after the transcontinental railroad was completed in 1869, and firearms were a necessary defense in the long stretches of uninhabited territory through which the stage lines had to pass. The movie "Stagecoach" in the 1930s, in which John Wayne was brought from obscurity to enduring fame, immortalized the vision of the attack by Native Americans. Another famous movie scenario was the stagecoach holdup by robbers, of which there were a considerable number. It is recorded that over the period 1870-1884 Wells Fargo suffered a total of 313 stage robberies, 34 attempted holdups, and annual losses of $30,000. Notorious holdup men included "Black Bart" (Charles E. Bolton) in California,

and William "Bill" Brazelton in the Arizona Territory.

The best-known vehicle used was the Concord Coach, introduced by the Abbott, Downing Company of Concord, New Hampshire, in 1827. It carried nominally nine passengers inside and another seven riding on top, plus the driver and a guard "riding shotgun," but sometimes even more would cram in, and sometimes there would be two guards. The shotguns shown here would be typical of the period, one of English manufacture with a full-length barrel, and an American gun evidently with the barrel shortened for close-in defense. Also shown is a Civil War Sharps carbine converted to use with metal cartridges also, interestingly, with its barrel shortened for defense purposes.

The Wells Fargo Company, then

and now also a major bank, established the first transcontinental stagecoach line in 1858, called the Butterfield Line after its president. At that time the United States was like two separate nations on the East and West coasts with a huge void in between; if everything went according to schedule, which it often did not, the stagecoach trip from the Mississippi River to California took three weeks.

Until the telegraph was completed in 1861, even communications went at that slow pace. For a year and a half before the telegraph was completed, the famous Pony Express cut the three weeks to ten days. The pistol shown here, a .36in caliber Whitney revolver, would have been a typical sidearm. Western figures such as "Buffalo Bill" Cody and "Wild

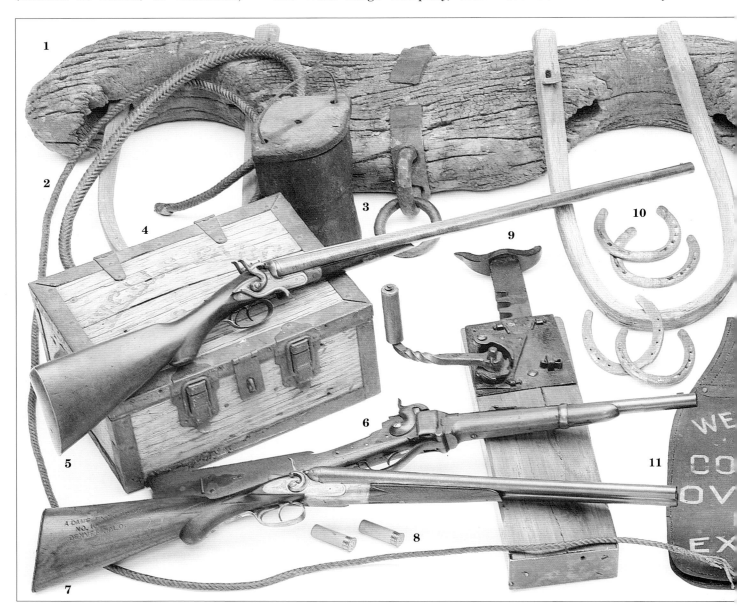

Above: *Colt's Model 1849 Pocket Revolver; the cylinder scene showing a passenger fighting off seven stagecoach robbers was somewhat ambitious, since the Model 1849 had a relatively low muzzle energy and was evidently intended for use at shorter ranges.*

Bill" Hickok were associated with the Pony Express (although Cody was not a rider, as he claimed).

There is an interesting bit of Colt advertising engraved on the cylinder of the Model 1849 Pocket Model percussion pistol and its successor of 1861: a scene showing a stagecoach robbery and a passenger shooting his revolver. He has downed three of the assailants, is shooting a fourth, and three more are hastily beating a retreat. The advertisement must have been successful, since Colt's sold about 325,000 of this model, the largest number of any of the company's percussion pistols.

A number of stagecoach passengers probably carried this pistol, but the guards would actually have used more powerful handguns and longarms, as described above.

KEY:
1. Wooden yoke for oxen, and ox bow, one of two on each yoke.
2. Driver's bullwhip.
3. Wooden grease or lubricant bucket for wagon wheels and axles.
4. Wood iron-bound strong box painted with logo "Wells Fargo."
5. Breech-loading sidehammer double-barrel shotgun made by J. B. Clabrough and Bro., London, 12-gauge.
6. Sharps new Model 1859 carbine with special order 15-inch barrel, .52 caliber, for Wells Fargo, for protection of coaches.
7. Breech-loading sidehammer double-barrel shotgun with short barrels made by Rhode Island Field Gun Company; 12-gauge. Stock marked "Adams Express Co., No. 10, Denver, Colo."
8. Two brass base shot shells for 12-gauge shotgun.
9. Iron and wood wagon jack.
10. Iron mule shoes.
11. Painted canvas saddle bags used by Wells Fargo & Company Overland Pony Express.
12. Whitney Navy revolver, .36 caliber, in open top "Slim Jim" holster.
13. Pony Express saddle with mochila, which fitted over the saddle and had four locked compartments integral to body.
14. Metal advertisement sign for Pony Express.

COWBOY GUNMEN

The first cowboys were from Texas, where the organized cattle industry in the United States began. Cattle and horses were first brought into North America by Cortez and the Spanish, and by the time the Alamo fell in 1836 there were an estimated 100,000 head of cattle running wild, which provided a major resource and incentive for the Texans to try to gain independence from Mexico. Small cattle drives to the East were organized before the Civil War, with the help of experienced Mexican "vaqueros" or cowboys, but in 1867 Joseph G. McCoy persuaded the Union Pacific Railroad to construct a switch or siding at a little place called Abilene, Kansas, to receive cattle from Texas. With former Confederate and Union soldiers and other unemployed workers available to work on ranches and cattle drives, business flourished, and more "cowtowns" were established. By 1871, 600,000 to 700,000 cattle a year were being moved north. It is estimated that some 35,000 cowboys took part in these drives from 1868 to 1895. One-third were Negroes and Mexicans, and the pay averaged only $30 per month. The big cattle drives ended effectively with a drop in meat prices in the 1890s and the extension of railroads into Texas.

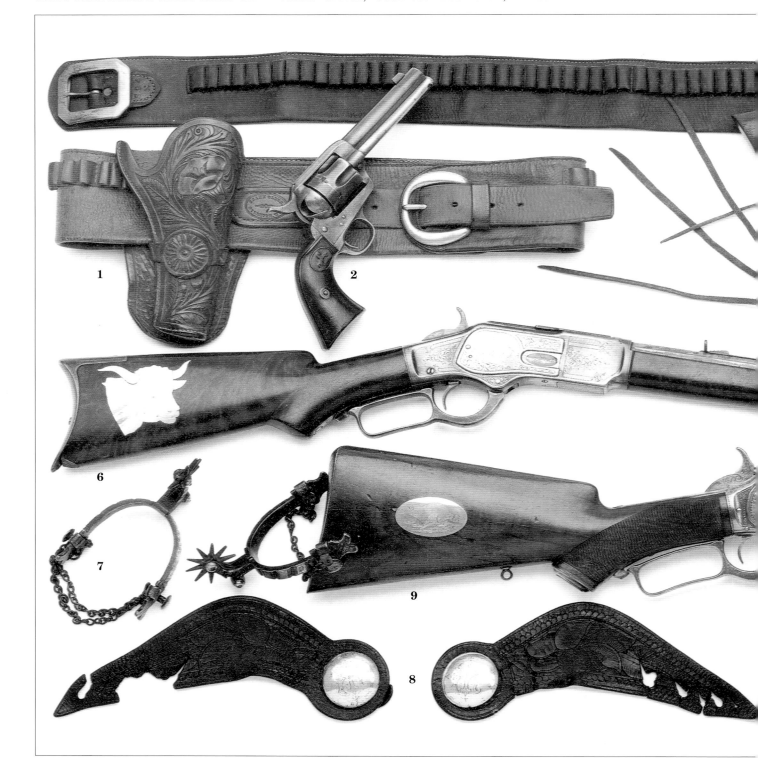

(Artifacts courtesy of Gene Autry Western Heritage Museum, Los Angeles, California.)

Apparently many cowboys did carry revolvers as in the romantic depiction in Western movies, but they were rarely used in range wars and other conflicts. Texas cowboys were known for showing off their revolvers in town after a two to three month trail drive, and shooting them in the air as a celebration, particularly after hitting the local saloons. Out on the range, cowboys carried revolvers for a variety of practical reasons. They were used to put injured animals out of their misery, were handy for deal-

KEY:

1. *Hand-tooled holster and cartridge belt which doubled as a money belt, c. 1900, used by George Gardiner, a working cowboy.*
2. *Colt Single Action, .38-40 caliber, carried by George Gardiner in the above holster.*
3. *Typical holster of about 1880, made by R. E. Rice, Dodge City.*
4. *Colt .44-40 Frontier Single Action revolver of about 1885.*
5. *Rawhide hand-braided riata, late 1800s.*
6. *Factory engraved and pearl-inlaid Winchester rifle Model 1873, owned by Charles Goodnight.*
7. *California-style silver-mounted spurs used by Theodore Roosevelt.*
8. *Spur straps with engraved "TR" conchos, probably made by J. S. Collins in Cheyenne, Wyoming, and used by Roosevelt in the Dakotas, late 1880s.*
9. *Roosevelt's Winchester Model 1876 carbine.*
10. *Engraved six-shooter with carved ivory grips carried in the West by Roosevelt. It represents his vision of the typical cowboy revolver but does not quite fit the bill.*
11. *Cheyenne-made holster, fitted to TR's revolver in about 1886.*

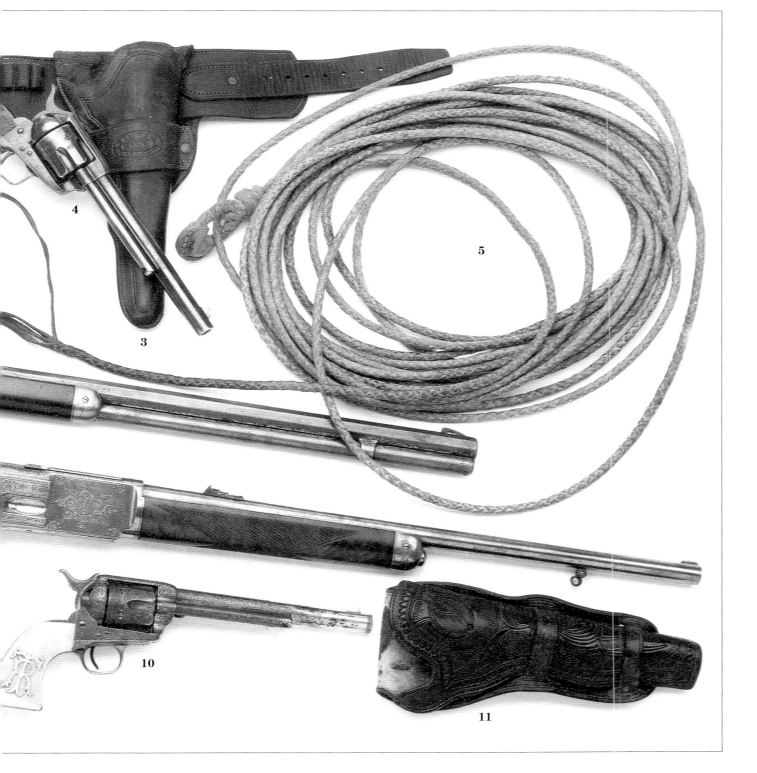

ing with snakes and rabid animals, and with a really lucky shot could help to put meat on the dinner table. Revolvers were also worn for reasons of status, but the truth is that they were also heavy and got in the way. The Colt Single Action Army revolvers shown here are typical of those used by the cowboys.

Rifles and carbines, which some of the cowboys carried in saddle scabbards or in their baggage, were valuable for hunting game and for defense against Native Americans and outlaws, who themselves would be armed with pistols and rifles. The Winchester Model 1873 rifle shown is a deluxe model owned by Charles Goodnight who, in 1866 in partnership with Oliver Loving, blazed the Goodnight-Loving trail to Fort Sumner and on to Colorado.

The Model 1876 carbine and the engraved, ivory-handled Colt revolver are another story. These belonged to Theodore Roosevelt and are from several expeditions he made to the Dakota Badlands, where he bought two large ranches. His hunting prowess was legendary, even though his eyesight was poor. He favored Winchesters; the fact that a Winchester could be sighted and fired, and fired again without having to remove the gun from his shoulder would have been a welcome feature.

Roosevelt also enjoyed dressing like a Westerner, albeit somewhat flamboyantly in the manner described as a "dude" – fringed and embroidered shirt and buckskin pants, with a wide-brimmed "Boss-of-the-Plains" Stetson – every bit that every dime novelist depicted as the hapless greenhorn. However, he quickly disabused anyone who tried

Above, left: *Some cowboys might have tried to look tougher or tidier in posed photographs such as this than they did on the range, but here their choice of clothing is correct. Weapons were for more practical day-to-day purposes, such as dealing with snakes and other wild animals, rather than in the very occasional range wars as romanticized by movie-makers.*

Left: *Cowhands enjoy the chow from an old-time chuckwagon, c. 1885. Said to have been perfected by cattle trailblazer Charles Goodnight, it had to be durable enough to survive the trail. The chuck box at the rear was Goodnight's special innovation*

to take advantage of this, and he made friends with many of the real Westerners.

The famous Texas gunman John Wesley Hardin, mentioned earlier, made the drive to Abilene as a trail boss in 1871, and on the way killed eight men in a dispute with Mexicans conducting another herd. There is no evidence, however, that many cowboys were as proficient or dangerous with the gun as Hardin.

Above: *A large proportion of cowboys (sometimes as many as twenty-five percent) were black, from a variety of backgrounds. Though some might have been former slaves, they apparently experienced little or no prejudice from white cowhands on the range.*

THE MILITARY UNTIL 1871

In what was known as the Dark Age of the American Army, its size was greatly reduced after the Civil War. There were only some 20,000 troops, occupying some 110 posts and forts protecting the settlers along the Western frontier. At the same time, there were some 200,000 Native Americans in the area, of which some 50,000 were overtly hostile. The soldier was always greatly outnumbered; daily he confronted fear, fatigue, poor rations and little appreciation from those he tried to protect.

All the types of pistols and lon-garms shown here, with the exception of the Allin conversion rifle, were left over from the Civil War and used by the postwar Army in the West. The Aston pistol was from before the war; it fired a large .54in caliber ball, but was a smoothbore accurate only at short range. Its attached ramrod facilitated loading, but even with a pair of these pistols in saddle holsters a mounted trooper would have only two shots available in a charge.

The revolvers shown, by Colt and Remington, were the standard cavalry issue during the Civil War. The heavy Colt Dragoon was replaced by the Model 1860 Army, which fired the same .44in caliber round. The shoulder stocks shown added accuracy and range to the revolvers, but were scarce and not standard issue (and are now highly prized as collectors' items).

The Sharps carbine was one of the most effective and widely used cavalry longarms of the Civil War. After the war, in 1867, the Army had about 31,000 of these converted to use .50in centerfire metallic cartridges, with liners being inserted in the barrels

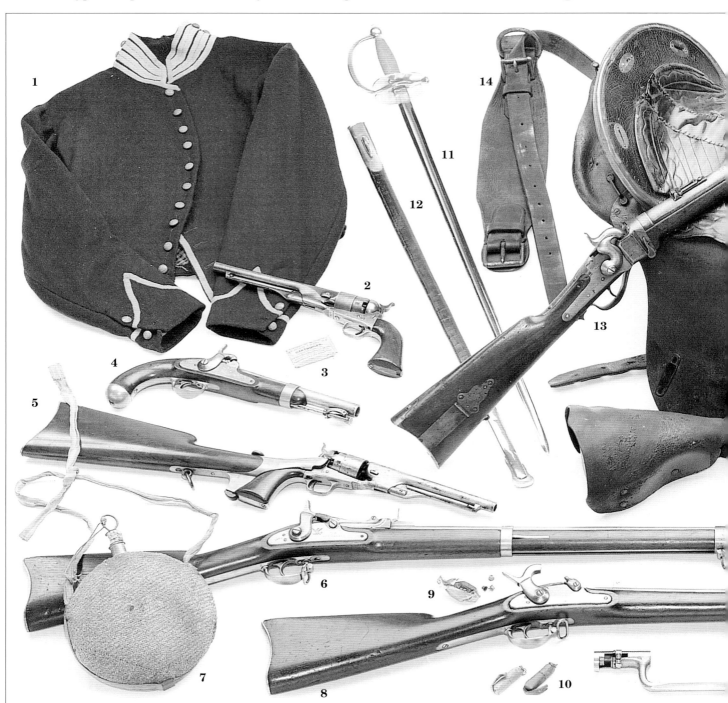

KEY:

1. Cavalry enlisted man's shell jacket, yellow indicating the branch of service.
2. Colt Model 1860 Army revolver, .44 caliber.
3. Pack of six .44 caliber combustible paper cartridges for above.
4. Model 1842 Aston single-shot pistol, .54 caliber.
5. Colt Model 1860 Army revolver, .44 caliber, with detachable shoulder stock affixed for use as a carbine.
6. Model 1865 first model Allin alteration rifle, .58 caliber.
7. Model 1858 tin canteen with cotton sling.
8. Model 1861 contract rifle musket, .58 caliber.
9. Paper-wrapped copper percussion caps for above.

10. .58 caliber paper cartridges; left standard, right Williams Patent Cleaner round, for (8).
11. Model 1840 non-commissioned officer's sword.
12. Brass-mounted leather scabbard for above.
13. Sharps Model 1859 breechloading carbine, .54 caliber.
14. Saddle cinch for (15).
15. Model 1859 brass-bound officer's McClellan saddle, with padded seat.
16. Colt Model 1851 Navy revolver, .36 caliber.
17. Pack of six .36 caliber combustible paper cartridges for above.
18. Model 1850 staff and field officer's sword.
19. Brass-mounted metal scabbards for above.

20. Artillery enlisted man's shell jacket, red indicating the branch of service.
21. Model 1858 infantry forage cap or kepi, the brass horn indicating branch of service.
22. Colt Third Model Dragoon revolver, .44 caliber, with detachable shoulder stock affixed for use as a carbine.
23. Colt Model 1851 Navy revolver, .36 caliber.
24. Remington New Model Army revolver, .44 caliber.
25. Model 1855 triangular socket bayonet for (8).
26. Brass-mounted scabbard for (25).
27. Wooden tompion to keep moisture out of the barrels of items (6) and (8).
28. Model 1855 cartridge box with shoulder belt. The box holds forty rounds of .58 caliber ammunition, such as item (10).

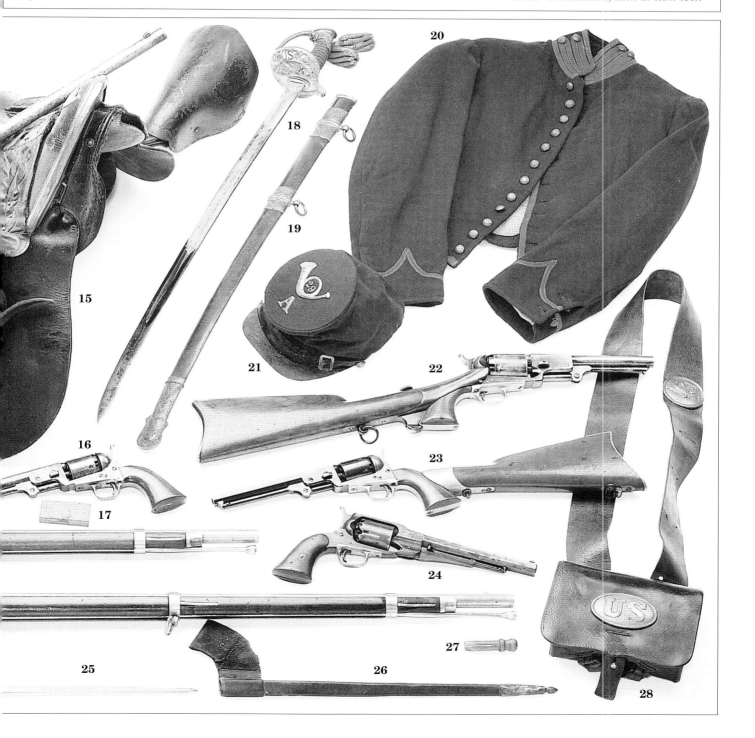

(the original version was in .52in caliber, using paper or linen cartridge and percussion caps). Many of these would have been issued to the Western cavalry.

The Springfield type rifle musket shown here was the standard Union issue in the Civil War, with over 1,000,000 made by the Springfield Armory and private contractors. The Army finally realized, by the end of the war, that breechloaders were better than muzzleloaders (although U.S. Ordnance had not yet recognized

the advantages of repeating over single-shot rifles), and in 1865 the superintendent of the Springfield Armory, Erskine Allin, devised a system of converting the percussion Springfield rifles to breechloaders using metallic cartridges. The result was the First Model Allin shown here, in .58 caliber rimfire.

The Allin system was improved in 1866 with a better extraction mechanism and the .50-70 centerfire cartridge, and this model, with a modification in 1868, were produced in a

quantity of some 60,000. In 1870 some 10,000 carbines of this type were produced. Again, barrel liners were used to accept the newer cartridge.

The new breechloading rifles came as a revelation to soldiers used to nothing but muzzleloaders. In contrast to the Fetterman Massacre of 1866 near Fort Phil Kearny, where Sioux Indians destroyed a troop of eighty-one cavalrymen armed with the old Springfield muzzleloaders, troops armed with the new

Above: *Sharps "New Model" 1859 breechloading carbine with backsight in the raised position. Over the years some 1,000 Sharps carbines were ordered.*

Above: *Maynard 1st Model carbine, an unusual type of carbine in which the lever action released a lock so that the gun could be "broken" (as shown here) to allow the weapon to be reloaded.*

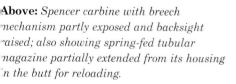

Above: *Spencer carbine with breech mechanism partly exposed and backsight raised; also showing spring-fed tubular magazine partially extended from its housing in the butt for reloading.*

breechloaders held off larger numbers of Native Americans in the "Hayfield Fight" near Fort Smith, and the "Wagon Box Fight" near Fort Phil Kearny.

Other arms from Union arsenals in the Civil war were undoubtedly used by the troops on the Western frontier, and new experimental models also were sent West to be tried out. There was a whole series of cavalry carbines made for the military by private manufacturers during the war, many with innovative features, such as the Maynard, pictured here, made by the Massachusetts Arms

Company. In addition to the Sharps and Spencer models as described above, the Joslyn carbine was converted to a rifle; the Remington Rolling Block rifle was made under contract, particularly for the Navy; and a short-lived single-shot, bolt action rifle, the Ward-Burton, was made in 1871.

In regard to handguns, Smith & Wesson in Springfield, Massachusetts, had a monopoly on cartridge revolvers until 1870, due to its control of the Rollin White patent on the bored through cylinder. Its .32in caliber Model 2 Army tip-up revolver was introduced at the beginning of the Civil War, but in spite of its name was not adopted by the Army. It was used extensively by the soldiers by private purchase, a practice which continued in the West after the war. However, in 1870 Smith & Wesson introduced a new larger revolver designed for military use, the top break .44in caliber, called the New Model American, modified as the Schofield. The Army promptly ordered 1,000 of these, and it was used by the cavalry until the adoption of the Colt Single Action Army in 1873.

Below: *Private Truman Head (known as "California Joe") armed with a Sharps .52in caliber rifle. He served with the 1st Regiment, U.S. Sharpshooters, also known as Berdan's Sharpshooters after its commanding officer, Colonel Hiram Berdan.*

THE MILITARY 1872-1890

The arms available to the Army and its cavalry in the West improved markedly starting around 1872. With regard to handguns, we have described how Colt's, after a delay waiting for the Rollin White patent for the bored-through cylinder to expire, came out with the Single Action Army revolver with a .45in self-contained cartridge in 1873, accepted by the Army after competitive trials. Under the name Peacemaker, this became the most famous handgun of the Old West. A competitor was the Smith & Wesson New Model American revolver introduced in 1870, and later the improved Schofield Model in 1875. This had the advantage of automatically ejecting the used cartridges when the barrel pivoted down, but was considered more complicated and not as sturdy as the Colt.

As also described earlier, the Spencer repeating carbine, with its eight-shot magazine loading through the butt, saw effective service in the Civil War. Some 11,000 of these were altered at the Springfield Armory after the war to .50in caliber from .52in, and many were issued in the West. However, these were replaced in 1873 when the more powerful .45-70 centerfire cartridge was developed. After trials with other single-shot rifles such as the Berdan (which was probably better), a new Springfield rifle and carbine using this cartridge was adopted. It was similar to the previous Allin conversion of the Civil War rifles, a "trapdoor" breech mechanism.

The change was unfortunate for George Armstrong Custer, who was lost with his entire command at the battle of the Little Bighorn in 1876. The single-shot carbines lacked the firepower of repeating rifles and also had extraction problems with their cartridges. If the troop had been armed with Winchester rifles or even Spencer carbines, the outcome might have been different (especially if the Gatling gun, which was available, had been brought along).

Inventor George Gatling's rapid-fire gun was developed as early as 1863, and saw limited service toward the end of the Civil War under General Benjamin Butler. It contained a group of up to ten barrels rotating around a central axis firing consecutively by

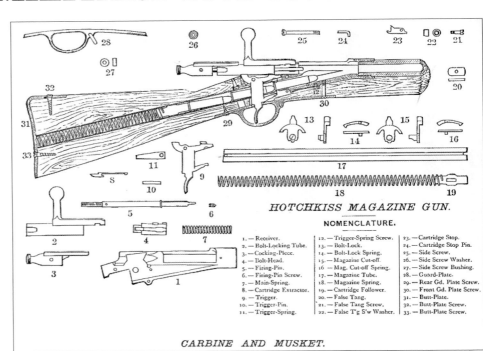

HOTCHKISS MAGAZINE GUN.

NOMENCLATURE.

1. — Receiver.	12. — Trigger-Spring Screw.	23. — Cartridge Stop.
2. — Bolt-Locking Tube.	13. — Bolt-Lock.	24. — Cartridge Stop Pin.
3. — Cocking-Piece.	14. — Bolt-Lock Spring.	25. — Side Screw.
4. — Bolt-Head.	15. — Magazine Cut-off.	26. — Side Screw Washer.
5. — Firing-Pin.	16. — Mag. Cut-off Spring.	27. — Side Screw Bushing.
6. — Firing-Pin Screw.	17. — Magazine Tube.	28. — Guard-Plate.
7. — Main-Spring.	18. — Magazine Spring.	29. — Rear Gd. Plate Screw.
8. — Cartridge Extractor.	19. — Cartridge Follower.	30. — Front Gd. Plate Screw.
9. — Trigger.	20. — False Tang.	31. — Butt-Plate.
10. — Trigger-Pin.	21. — False Tang Screw.	32. — Butt-Plate Screw.
11. — Trigger-Spring.	22. — False T'g S'w Washer.	33. — Butt-Plate Screw.

CARBINE AND MUSKET.

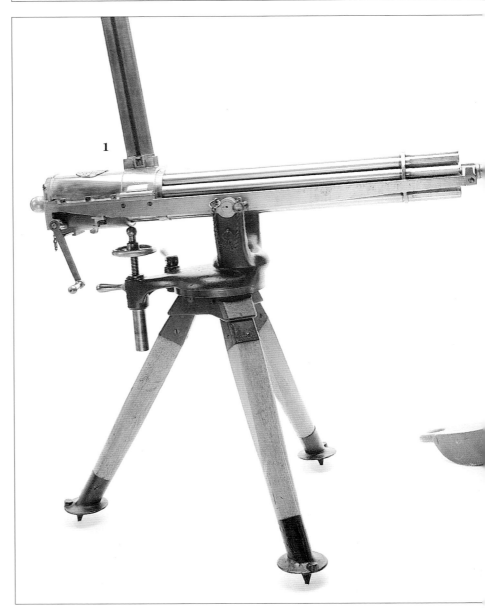

Far left: *The Hotchkiss rifle (shown in the Winchester catalog of 1882) was ordered by the Army. It had six shots in the butt, loaded from the top of the receiver. The bolt handle extended out to the side, and was worked by turning to the vertical position and pulling back to cock and to eject a used cartridge, then pushing forward and turning to load a fresh cartridge and lock the action.*

Left: *Gatling's Model 1875 being test-fired at Colt's. It is mounted on a wheeled carriage (total weight 444lb). Cyclic rate was about 800rpm. Gun length was 59.4in; barrel length, 31.9in. It used standard Army .45in caliber cartridges gravity fed from a box magazine mounted on top of the bronze breech housing. The barrels were mechanically rotated and fired using a lever on the right-hand side of the weapon.*

KEY:

1. Gatling gun, Model 1875, on wooden tripod with crude elevating mechanism, ammunition magazine in place, operated by the hand crank seen extended below breech.
2. Hotchkiss two-pounder breech loading mountain gun. Light artillery piece.
3. 1.65in. canister round for above.
4. 1.65in. common explosive shell for above.

KEY:

1. Forage cap, about 1889.
2. Model 1883 five-button sack coat.
3. Model 1874 U.S. belt.
4. Model 1880 Springfield armory hunting knife and scabbard.
5. Springfield Model 1884 breechloading rifle.
6. Model 1881 canteen.
7. Smith and Wesson First Model Schofield revolver.
8. Box of .45 caliber ammunition for (7).
9. Colt Model 1894 Double Action revolver.
10. Box of .38 caliber ammunition for (9).
11. Spencer Model 1865 repeating carbine.
12. Magazine tube inserted in butt of (11).
13. Ammunition for (11), (12).
14. Model 1860 cavalry saber.
15. Metal scabbard for (14).
16. Brass bugle.
17. McClellan saddle.
18. Colt Single Action Army revolver, .45 caliber.
19. Two boxes of .45 caliber ammunition for (18).
20. Riding gauntlets.
21. Scabbard for (22).
22. Entrenching bayonet.
23. Scabbard for Model 1873 triangular socket bayonet.
24. Model 1885 carbine boot.
25. Springfield Model 1884 carbine, .45-70 caliber.
26. Box of .45-70 caliber ammunition.
27. Brass spurs, about 1872.
28. Monocular or telescope.
29. Cavalry dress helmet.
30. Cavalry officer's campaign hat.
31. Cavalry officer's forage cap, 10th Cavalry, 1874.
32. Leather monocular case.
33. Cavalry breeches, c.1890.

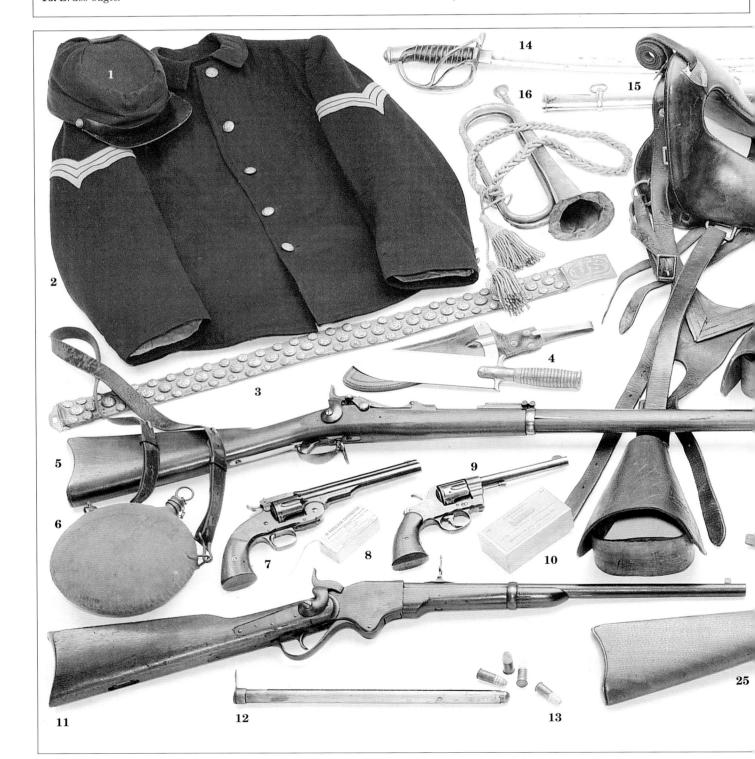

means of a hand crank mechanism. The Model 1875 made by Colt's was adopted by the Army and was present in most Western garrisons; Custer did not take the guns on his expedition because he felt they would slow his progress.

Another major weapon was adopted late in the Old West period, the Hotchkiss two-pounder cannon. Based on a French design, it was adopted in 1885, and was used at the Battle of Wounded Knee (also referred to as a massacre of Native Americans by the Army), the last engagement of the Indian Wars. It had a range of 4,000 yards, and the Native Americans had no defense against it.

Up to 1894 the standard Army rifle and carbine was the single-shot trapdoor Springfield using the .45-70 cartridge, with minor variations up to the Model 1888. However, the Springfield Armory experimented with bolt action repeating rifles, such as the 1882 Chaffee Reese, loading through the butt. A more successful attempt at a bolt action repeating rifle was made by Winchester with its Hotchkiss model, introduced in 1879, again loading through the butt. Some 2,400 of these were made for the Army at the Springfield Armory, with an additional quantity made by Winchester.

The Army's single-shot .45-70 rifle was pushed further into obsolescence by developments in Europe, where in 1886 the French made an infantry rifle using smokeless powder, followed by the German Mannlicher rifle in 1888, which loaded from a clip fed magazine. The U.S. Army did not catch up until 1894, when it adopted the Krag-Jorgensen rifle with the .30-40 cartridge.

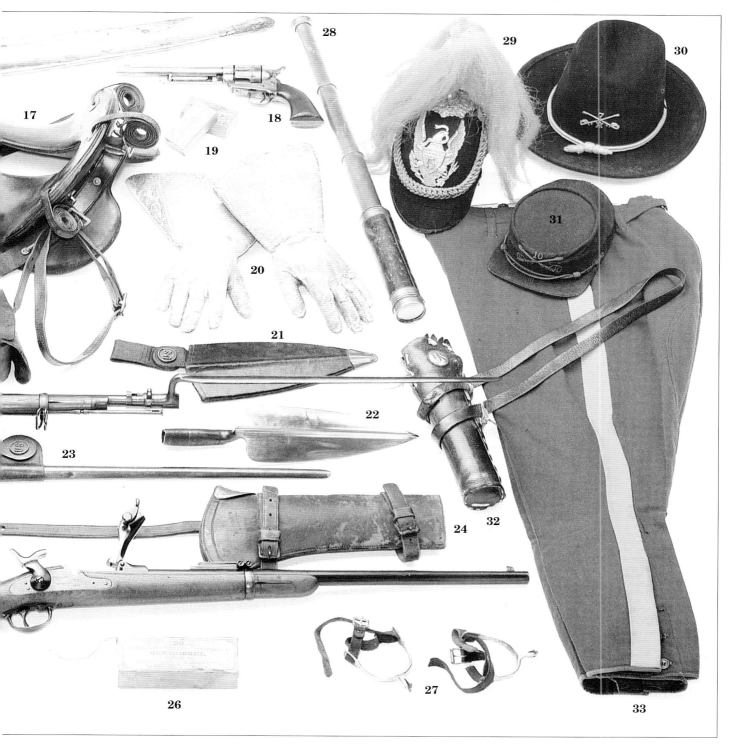

FIREARMS OF THE NATIVE AMERICANS

The Native Americans by necessity used firearms acquired from the whites. From the earliest fur trading days, they were impressed with the efficiency of firearms compared with the native weapons of bows and arrows, axes and clubs, and lances. For many Native Americans, warfare between the tribes was a way of life, a way to prove manhood; and for all the Native Americans the advantages of firearms for hunting game soon became apparent.

Typical trade guns were obsolete flintlock and percussion muzzleloading arms. Many were made in England as well as America for the purpose of trading with the Native Americans. There was even a U.S. Government short flintlock musket known as the Indian Carbine made by the Springfield Armory between 1807 and 1810, in a total quantity of 1,202. This was under order of the Indian Department, as gifts for friendly Native Americans. Extant examples of this weapon are highly prized by collectors.

Breechloading arms were acquired by the Native Americans in raids on or battles with white settlers and the Army, but they had no source of supply once the ammunition was expended. Examples have been found in which loose powder and ball were used as substitutes for fixed ammunition. The Indian kept his arms functional long after a white owner would have discarded and arms as useless, and he was a master of adaptation and ingenuity in this regard.

Arms used by the Native Americans are typically identified by their use of brass tacks as ornamentation, as shown in the accompanying

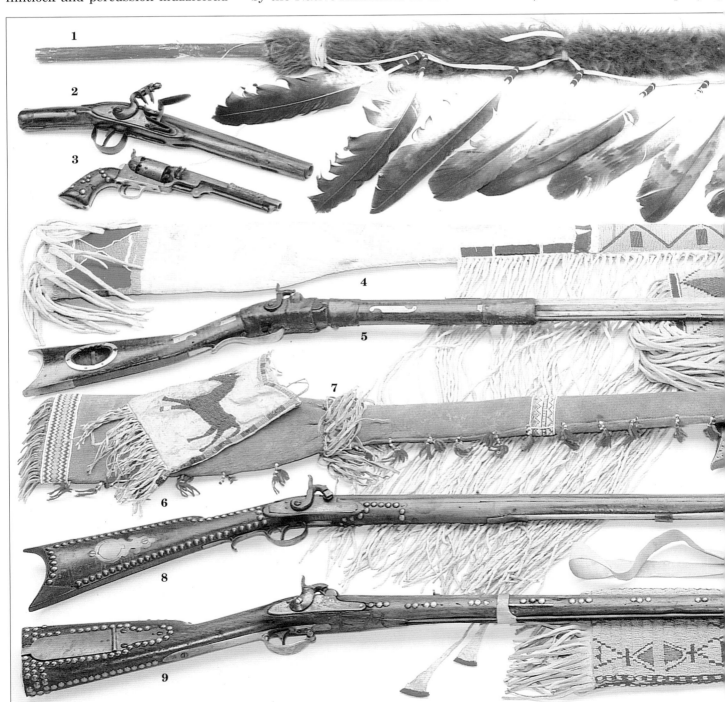

KEY:

1. *Crow chief's staff, representing a flag.*
2. *Flintlock pistol, made from cutdown trade musket, .50 caliber.*
3. *Colt Model 1851 Navy revolver with brass tack repair, .36 caliber.*
4. *Crow rifle scabbard, hand-tanned buffalo hide.*
5. *Unmarked percussion single-shot rifle. Note rawhide repairs around lock area and rear of barrel. .45 caliber.*
6. *Sioux ammunition pouch, with beaded blue horse.*
7. *Santee Sioux rifle scabbard, hand-tanned smoked deerskin.*
8. *Percussion single-shot trade rifle. Brass tacks decorate stock; about .40 caliber.*
9. *U.S. Model 1841 percussion rifle.*
10. *North plains ammunition pouch, buckskin or elk hide.*
11. *Flintlock trade musket.*
12. *Crow ammunition pouch.*
13. *Cheyenne or Santee Sioux ammunition pouch, may be elk hide.*
14. *Sioux Ghost Dance pouch.*
15. *Crow rifle scabbard.*
16. *Ballard breechloading sporting rifle, dual ignition system, with altered forestock and brass tack decoration.*
17. *Winchester Model 1866 carbine, with added brass tack design.*
18. *Oglala Sioux rifle scabbard, hand-tanned elk skin.*

illustration. Also, the stocks were often repaired or reinforced with rawhide. Where there is a reasonable provenance dating back to the Old West era, these arms again are sought after by collectors.

The significance of the chief's staff in the accompanying illustration is that when gifts or trades took place, it was the chief, rather than the warriors, who first received the arms from the whites.

The Native Americans under Sitting Bull and Crazy Horse, who wiped out Custer's command, are known to have had a number of modern rifles of that time, such as

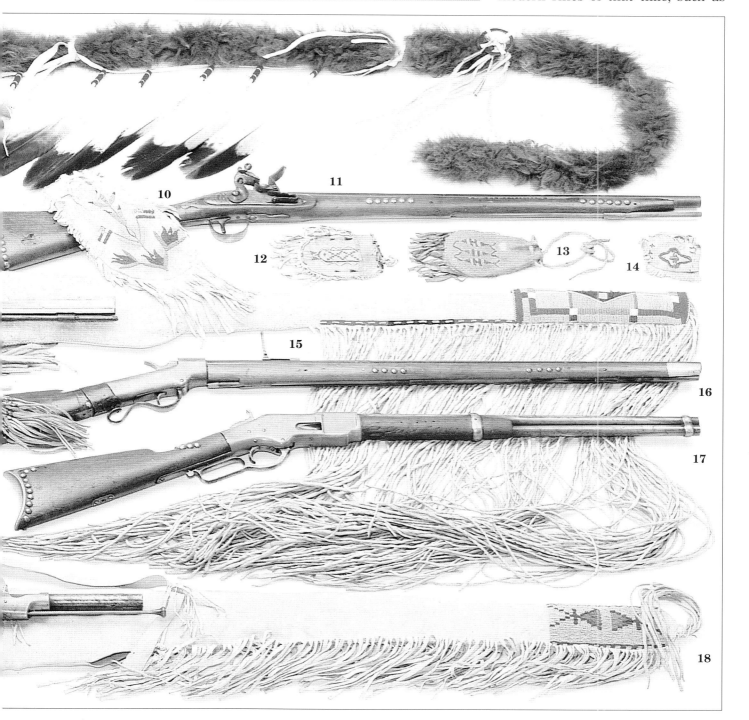

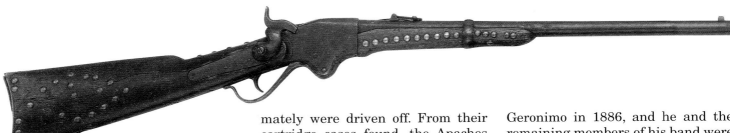

Above: *A U.S. Army Spencer carbine (serial number 30670) in .56-56 military caliber, as carried at the battle of the Little Bighorn by a Cheyenne warrior.*

the Ballard and Winchester shown here. A recent archaeological survey of a battlefield from four years after the Little Bighorn, in New Mexico, gives a startling picture of the range of firearms used by the Native Americans.

The battle was part of the two-year Victorio War, named for the chief of a band of Chiricahula Apaches who lost their promised reservation and were forced by the Indian Bureau to share land with several other Apache bands. The battle took place in the Hembrillo Basin between Victorio's band and the Ninth Cavalry, which was composed of black troops or "Buffalo Soldiers" under white officers. The Apaches surrounded the regiment, but ulti-

mately were driven off. From their cartridge cases found, the Apaches had Henry rifles and Model 1873 Winchesters as well as .45-70 and .50-70 Springfields, plus long-range Remingtons and Sharps. The cavalrymen used only the regulation Springfield carbines and Colt revolvers.

The most famous encounter between the Army and the Native Americans after Custer's defeat at the Little Bighorn was the five year campaign to stop Geronimo, the Apache chief from the San Carlos reservation in Arizona where ranchers from Tombstone supplied beef at the time of the gunfight at the O.K. Corral. With a substantial sized band of warriors and their families, Geronimo first broke out of the reservation in 1881, the same year as the famous gunfight. He was brought in for peace talks by General George Crook, considered the greatest of Indian fighters, but slipped away the night before the treaty was to have been concluded. Troops under General Miles finally captured

Geronimo in 1886, and he and the remaining members of his band were deported to Florida. As shown by the accompanying illustration, Geronimo's warriors were primarily armed with military single-shot rifles and Winchester repeaters.

Many Native Americans served as scouts for the Army, as police on the reservations, and even as auxiliary troops. General Crook's successful expedition against Crazy Horse and 6,000 Sioux and Cheyenne at the Rosebud River in Montana in 1876 included 250 friendly Indian troops, besides his 1,000 regulars. Special arms were sometimes issued to the Indian Police, such as nickel-plated Smith & Wesson Schofield revolvers.

Right: *Geronimo (far right) in 1886, with a .45-70 trapdoor Springfield; his brother-in-law Yanozha (far right) with Winchester 1873 carbine; son Chappo with another 1873 carbine; and second cousin Fun with .45-70 Springfield carbine.*

Below: *The Chiricahua Apache Geronimo with his fearsome band of renegades in 1886.*

W. F. CODY AND THE WILD WEST SHOWS

William F. "Buffalo Bill" Cody and his Wild West show are associated with the end of the Old West, which can be dated in the vicinity of 1890. Certainly his "Wild West" (he did not use the word "show") played until 1917 and helped create exaggerated myths of the Old West, but he started his career as a showman as early as 1872, when he starred in Ned Buntline's play "The Scouts of the Prairie."

Cody's colorful career began as a messenger boy (not an actual rider) for the Pony Express in 1860-61. He joined the Union Army during the Civil War, and afterward worked for the Army as a scout and dispatch rider. For eight months he worked as a hunter for the Kansas Pacific Railroad (part of the Union Pacific),

downing more than 4,000 buffalo (later regretting this as the buffalo neared extinction). He continued to serve as an Army scout and guide from 1868 to 1876, taking part in many Indian campaigns and winning a Medal of Honor. Between seasons he guided hunting parties of European nobility. The full story of his career, and many artifacts related to it, are preserved in the Buffalo Bill Historical Center in Cody, Wyoming, a town which he founded, near the entrance to Yellowstone National Park. Cody's show, "Buffalo Bill's Wild West and Congress of Rough Riders of the World," employed actual frontiersmen and Native Americans for spectacles such as Indian war dances and an attack on a stagecoach. Cody himself took

part in shooting exhibitions, along with the famous Annie Oakley, "Little Sure Shot." Imitators with their own shows included Pawnee Bill (Gordon William Lillie), who began with Cody's show, formed his own, and then merged back with Cody in 1908.

Among Cody's firearms shown here, representative of the many that he owned, some were presented to him, while some he presented to others. The worn Springfield Model 1856 Allin Conversion rifle is especially significant. He called this his "Lucretia Borgia," and it was this rifle that he used during his buffalo hunting career.

The other firearms shown, a pair of Colt Single Action Army revolvers and a cased percussion Pocket

KEY:

1. *Tanned leather long coat with buffalo calf hide trim and fringe on sleeves, with colored beadwork and trade cloth decoration.*
2. *Gray felt wide-brim hat with silk hatband marked in sweatband "Stetson Co. 1224 Chestnut St, Philadelphia."*
3,4. *Pair of Colt Single Action Army revolvers with 7¹/₂ inch barrels, .44 caliber, nickeled finish with ivory grips, together with leather flap holsters lined with deer skin. The handguns were given by William F. Cody to W. F. Schneider in 1880.*
5. *Pair of Mexican silver-mounted spurs engraved "Wild West." The leather straps were embossed "Morrow & Thomas Hdwe. Co. Amarillo, Texas."*
6. *Winchester Model 1873 deluxe rifle, .44 caliber, factory engraved with select wood and gold-plated receiver.*
7. *Silver-mounted side knife and sheath made by William Rose, New York. Ivory handle is inlaid with two silver escutcheons engraved "W. F. Cody" and "Hays City, 1869."*
8. *Pair of percussion single-shot Deringers, .44 caliber. Silver escutcheons on each pistol are engraved "W. F. Cody 1865." Cody would have used cartridge Deringers not long after that.*
9. *Beaded white buckskin gauntlets, probably of Sioux origin.*
10. *Silver-mounted deluxe saddle, "Hon. W. F. Cody" inlaid in silver in the cantle. A silver plaque under the saddle horn is engraved "Collins & Morrison Makers, Omaha, Neb."*
11. *Silk top hat.*
12. *Masonic sword of Knights Templar, blade etched with Cody's name; and leather storage case for above, bearing legend "W. F. Cody North Platte, Nebr."*
13. *Brown leather cigar case with ink inscription on reverse "From Chief Bull to Buffalo Bill."*
14. *Gold watch made by the Elgin National Watch Co. The reverse is engraved "Presented to Edward Z. C. Judson" by his friend William F. Cody May 1885."*
15. *Cased, engraved Colt Model 1849 Pocket Model, a deluxe Winchester Model revolver, .31 caliber.*
16. *Tin of caps and gun wrench from cased set, item (15).*
17. *Relic Springfield Model 1866 Allin Alteration rifle, .58 caliber, named "Lucretia Borgia" by Cody and used by him to hunt buffalo for the railroad.*
18. *Medal of Honor, 1862 Pattern. The reverse of the medal is engraved "The Congress to William F. Cody, Guide, for Gallantry at Platte River, Nebr. April 26, 1872."*
19. *Formal black tailcoat.*
20. *Pair of black high top tie shoes.*
21. *Stock certificate of Buffalo Bill's Wild West show.*
22. *Gold watch with silver squirrel inlaid in front of case. The reverse is engraved "Buffalo Bill (Hon. W. F. Cody) to White Beaver (D. Frank Powell, MD) Life Long Pards 1884."*
23. *Gold-headed wooden cane, head engraved.*
24. *Chased gold-handled cane, engraved "Compliments of Jos. H. Horton to Buffalo Bill."*

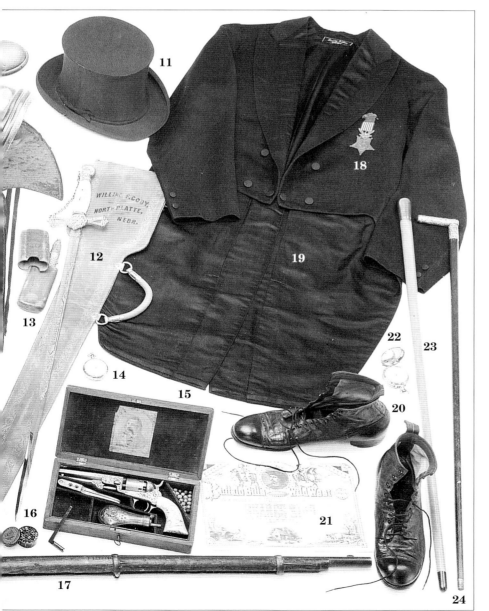

Model, a deluxe Winchester Model 1873 rifle, and a pair of Deringer pistols, are fine examples of weapons discussed in previous chapters. The entire Winchester Company factory collection is now in the Buffalo Bill Historical Center in Cody, Wyoming.

Annie Oakley was as well known as Buffalo Bill, and her fame came entirely from her skill with firearms. Born in Ohio in 1860, originally Phoebe Anne Oakley Moses, she became a champion target shooter while in her teens. While still young, as featured in the musical "Annie Get Your Gun," she defeated ranking marksman Frank E. Butler in a shooting match in Cincinnati, and the two successfully toured the vaudeville circuits and circuses until 1885. She then joined the Buffalo Bill Wild West show as "Miss Annie Oakley, the Peerless Lady Wing-Shot," with her husband serving as manager and attendant. Her specialties included hitting at 30 paces the thin edge of a playing card and a dime tossed in the air. There is some thought that she used a smoothbore rifle loaded with shot pellets, but she would also, at the same distance, shoot a cigarette out of her husband's lips. She and Frank stayed with the show for 17 years, and on one occasion, while touring Europe, she performed the cigarette trick with Crown Prince William of Germany, later the Kaiser, and there is speculation about what would

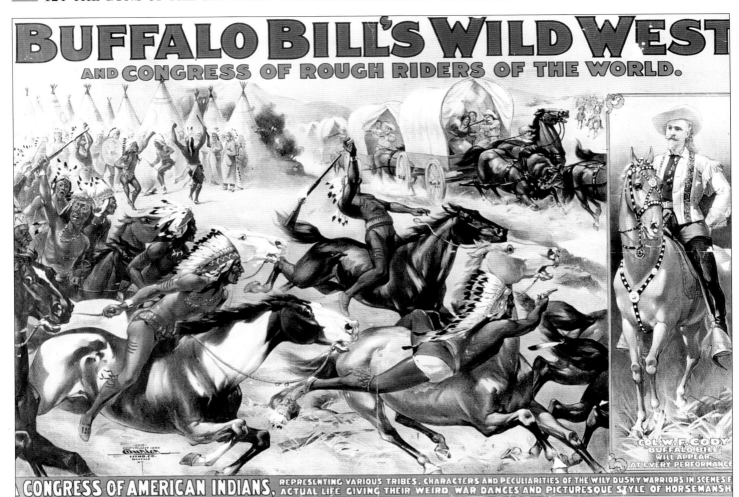

BUFFALO BILL'S WILD WEST
AND CONGRESS OF ROUGH RIDERS OF THE WORLD.

CONGRESS OF AMERICAN INDIANS, REPRESENTING VARIOUS TRIBES, CHARACTERS AND PECULIARITIES OF THE WILY DUSKY WARRIORS IN SCENES F ACTUAL LIFE GIVING THEIR WEIRD WAR DANCES AND PICTURESQUE STYLE OF HORSEMANSH

COL. W. F. CODY
"BUFFALO BILL"
WILL APPEAR
AT EVERY PERFORMANCE

Above: *Colorful poster advertising "Buffalo Bill's Wild West" show, illustrating the use of authentic Indians, some of them armed with Winchester rifles.*

Left: *William F. "Buffalo Bill" Cody in a promotional photograph taken in Paris in 1889. His Wild West show was popular in Europe as well as America.*

Right: *Annie Oakley with a deluxe, engraved Winchester Model 1892 rifle, with half-round, half-octagonal barrel. "Little Sure Shot" was a markswoman of the highest standard.*

have happened to World War I if she had missed and killed the Prince!

Oakley and Butler continued to give trapshooting lessons and demonstrations after 1901, when she was injured in a train wreck. She lived for a number of years in Nutley, New Jersey, and died in 1926. Her name became associated with a free theater or other entertainment ticket, which was known as an "Annie Oakley," because these tickets customarily had a hole punched in them, reminiscent of the small cards which Annie would shoot during her theatrical performances.

BARRY

BIBLIOGRAPHY

Austerman, Wayne R., "'Speaks Far Gun,' Sharps Rifles and the Plains Indians," in *Man at Arms* magazine, March-April, 1984.

Boorman, Dean K., *The History of Colt Firearms* (London: Salamander Books, 2001).
The History of Winchester Firearms (London: Salamander Books, 2001).

Bruce, Robert V., *Lincoln and the Tools of War* (Urbana, IL: University of Illinois Press, 1989).

Davis, William C., *The American Frontier* (Norman, OK, The University of Oklahoma Press, 1999, and Salamander

Books Ltd., London).

Davis, William C., and Rosa, Joseph G., eds., *The West* (London: Salamander Books, 1994).

Flayderman, Norm, *Flayderman's Guide to Antique American Firearms* (Iola, WI: Krause Publications, 1998).

Laumbach, Karl W., "Fire Fight at Hembrillo Basin," in *Archaeology Magazine*, November-December 2001.

Mayberry, Gerald R., "Buffalo Guns and Adobe Walls," in the *Bulletin* of the American Society of Arms Collectors, October, 1994.

McGivern, Ed, *Ed McGivern's Book of Fast and Fancy Revolver Shooting* (Boston, MA:

Williams Bookstore, 1945).

Rosa, Joseph G., *Age of the Gunfighter* (Norman, OK: University of Oklahoma Press, 1995, and Salamander Books, London)).
Guns of the American West (London: Lionel Leventhal Ltd., 1985).

Scarlata, Paul S., *Collecting Classic Bolt Action Military Rifles* (Lincoln, RI: Andrew Mowbray Publishers, 2001).

Walter, John, *The Guns That Won the West* (London: Greenhill Books, 1999).

Wilson, R. L., *Colt, an American Legend* (New York, NY: Abbeville Press, 1985).
Winchester, An American Legend (New York, NY: Random House, 1991).

INDEX